Firecracker Leadership

How to become a great leader

Sue Musson

R^ethink

First published in Great Britain in 2024
by Rethink Press (www.rethinkpress.com)

For Mike, Harry and Annabel with gratitude
for all the love and all the laughs

Contents

Introduction   1

    The secret of Firecracker Leadership   3
    Head, hands, heart in balance   5
    The Firecracker Leader   6
    The Firecracker Leadership Framework   9
    Taking stock   10

1 How To Inspire Others   13

    Inspiration – anyone can do it   14
    Overcoming the analysis gap   16
    Overcoming the communication gap   19
    Overcoming the humility gap   26
    Overcoming the confidence gap   34
    Summary   38

2 How To Set Purpose   41

    St Jude Children's Research Hospital   42
    Inspiration blockers   45

Making sense of complexity 49

Purpose outside healthcare 51

Summary 52

3 How To Build A Winning Team 55

Analysing the skill chessboard 57

Appealing to talent 58

Fair, wise recruitment practices 60

Warm welcomes 76

Sustaining the team 78

When it all goes horribly wrong 82

Summary 88

4 How To Celebrate Good Times 91

Using symbols 94

Showcasing key events 96

Building celebration and gratitude
into daily life 100

When highlighting the bad is good 102

Ephemera vs lasting impact 103

Summary 107

5 How To Cope With Crisis 109

Work disasters 110

Personal disasters 119

Big-scale disasters 125

Summary 129

6 How To Survive The Fishbowl   **133**

Learning from royalty   134

Other winning traits   142

At the other end of the spectrum   148

Role modelling   155

Gather feedback   158

Friendly, not friends   159

Summary   161

7 How To Stay Resilient   **163**

Programme yourself to cope with adversity   164

Goals create energy   167

Investing in you   170

Resilience boosters   175

Laughter is the best medicine   179

Summary   182

References   **185**

Further Reading   **189**

Acknowledgements   **193**

The Author   **195**

Introduction

You can probably call to mind immediately the teacher who had the biggest impact on you as a child. Without needing to dredge through your memory, you can conjure a mental picture of that teacher and recall exactly what they said or did that made such an impression on you. You know how your teacher made you feel at the time and how it still affects you today.

For many of you, that recollection may be a happy memory of a person in authority who spotted something positive in you and gave you a message that made you believe in your ability or potential, forming part of your confident self-image. For others, unfortunately, that may be a deeply unhappy memory of a stinging criticism or a belittling comment that made you feel inadequate at the time and still lingers with you today.

Leadership works in precisely the same way. Good leadership provides a catalyst to self-belief, confidence, growth and achievement. Poor leadership demotivates and creates negative feelings of anxiety, fear, resentment, inadequacy and paralysis.

Consider your own experience of good leadership and poor leadership from your working life. You can most likely do that with the same speed and clarity of recall as remembering the impact of a teacher from your past.

We are all a product of our beliefs and our experiences. Leadership skill is developed in exactly the same way. It is a by-product of beliefs and experiences and can be cultivated. The chapters of this book will share with you seven 'how tos' to help you become a better leader, a *Firecracker Leader*.

When I set up my consultancy business twenty-two years ago, I called it Firecracker Projects. To me, the name Firecracker conjures up something dynamic, eye-catching and exciting. Something that prompts an 'Ooooooh, ahhhh' when spotted. Since then, I have founded three organisations under the Firecracker brand, so it feels natural to describe great leadership as Firecracker Leadership.

I am excited to share with you the observations and insights I have gained over my thirty years' experience as a leader in senior executive and non-executive roles. I have been privileged to witness at first hand and to learn from some truly outstanding examples of leadership skill from remarkable individuals. I have seen the leadership talent of royalty in the form of their Royal Highnesses, the Prince and Princess of Wales, and of footballing royalty in the form of Jordan Henderson, former captain of Liverpool Football Club. I have witnessed extraordinary leadership from many ordinary people, too. Importantly, these exemplars demonstrate skills and abilities that are readily available to you to improve your own effectiveness as a great leader.

The secret of Firecracker Leadership

Many years ago, at the age of ten, my son Harry had a horrible life-threatening illness that meant he spent six weeks in hospital undergoing numerous surgeries. Fortunately, he made a full recovery, and being the positive, glass half-full soul that he is, he told me that it was a good thing he had had such a terrible experience because it led him to his vocation to become a doctor.

He said he thought he would be a good doctor because he knew what it felt like to be the patient in the bed. That was a profound insight for a ten-year-old.

Around the same time, I overheard him speaking to my dad, a retired surgeon himself. Harry asked, 'Grandpa, what makes a good doctor?'

My dad thought for a moment, then said, 'Harry, a good doctor owes it to his patients to give them the best of *this*, the best of *this* and, most of all, the best of *this*.' With the first this, he pointed to his head; with the second, he waggled his fingers; and with the third, he brought his fingers to his heart.

This: meaning the best of your brainpower.

This: meaning the best of your technical skill.

This: meaning the best of your ability to care with love and compassion.

That exchange has always stayed with me and is central to the philosophy of Firecracker Leadership.

The secret of great leadership is to harness the best of your brainpower, the best of your technical skill and the best of your ability to care with love and compassion – all in equal measure. Head. Hands. Heart. The foundation of great leadership occurs when these three areas are in abundance and in balance.

I am pleased to report that Harry did indeed follow his vocation and is now a fantastic doctor. He took on board my dad's advice and demonstrates every day his exceptional knowledge, technical skill and compassion, all to the benefit of his patients.

Head, hands, heart in balance

Can you think of leaders you have worked with who had some good qualities, but who did not represent all three areas of head, hands and heart in balance?

Perhaps you recall working with a leader who was completely focused on activity and performance goals, often seeing the emotional side of leadership as irrelevant or soft. These people tend to think that a telling, directive style is the best way to get results. Although this might work in the short term, this approach is often alienating – inducing fear, anxiety and resentment in others, rather than sustained high performance.

Maybe you recall working for a technocrat leader – the type of person who is proficient in a technical area, but deficient in developing wider knowledge or communicating with empathy. Sometimes, these individuals have been promoted to a managerial role based on their personal performance rather than having developed true leadership skills. While they may be admired for their technical skill, their impulse to say, 'Give it here' and complete everything personally can be off-putting. Their focus on their own competence can leave their teams experiencing a lack of either trust or encouragement to learn and develop.

Finally, what of the overly empathetic leader? These are leaders who have a wealth of compassion and understanding, but they are often reluctant to inject urgency, a clear direction or high expectations for results. They may be kind, agreeable people, but their teams are often left feeling directionless and frustrated.

Developing all three areas in balance is crucial for success if you wish to become an exceptional leader.

The Firecracker Leader

What does it look like when all three areas – head, hands, heart – are present and in balance? These are the indicators of great leadership:

Head	• Inspiring purpose and goals • Analytical skills • Solutions • Curiosity • Learning
Hands	• Technical skills • Good communication • Professionalism • Role modelling behaviours • Fair recruitment and reward

Heart 	• Integrity, honesty, compassion • Managing conflict and mistakes • Approachable and empathetic • Giving feedback • Encouraging teamwork and appreciation

Consider your own starting point as a leader and assess your proficiency in each of these areas: head, hands, heart. Is there an area of strength or weakness that stands out?

The following are some good questions to ask yourself to take stock of where you are right now.

Head

- What is the quality of your leadership knowledge and thinking?

- Are you up to date?

- Are you open to learning and continuous self-development?

- How self-aware are you?

- What is the quality of your self-talk, the voice inside your head?

- Are you feeding your subconscious mind a good diet to build a healthy self-image, confidence and effectiveness in yourself and others?

Hands

- What is the quality of your technical skill?

- Whatever your role or profession, are your technical and leadership skills current and up to scratch?

- Do you have the analytical skills you need to implement your vision?

- How effectively do you communicate with others?

- Now that you are a leader, do you think the doing side of the job is beneath you?

- Are you resting on your laurels or actively developing and improving your skills?

Heart

- What is the quality of your caring?

- How easy is it for you to express emotion?

- Are you regularly demonstrating empathy, compassion and concern for yourself and for others?

- Are you fearful of showing emotion and vulnerability?

- Do you perceive displays of emotion as weakness?

This book will share insights to help you master all three areas so you can achieve the best expression of your own leadership. The chapters include real-life examples of leadership. Some are good, some are bad and some are just ugly, but they are all equally applicable for the leader who wants to learn how to replicate good practice, avoid mistakes and reject poor practice.

Join me in my mission to eradicate imposter syndrome. Allow the more confident, intuitive and effective leader within you to emerge.

I wish you the best of luck in your leadership journey. No doubt, you will have great times and trying times. That is a given in life, but do remember that every leadership experience is an opportunity to capture and repeat the good and to learn from the bad.

As Napoleon Hill wrote, 'Every adversity, every failure, every heartache carries with it the seed of an equal or greater benefit.'[1]

Enjoy the ride!

The Firecracker Leadership Framework

The Firecracker Leadership Framework sets out fifteen must-have skills and abilities. The Firecracker Leader possesses all of these in abundance and in balance.

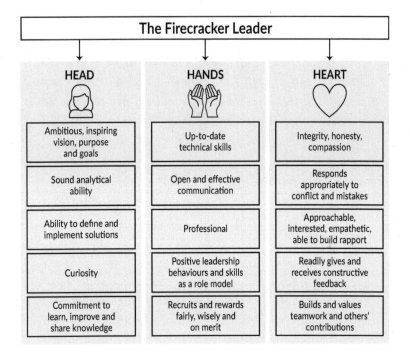

Taking stock

What is your start point? Assess where you are on each of the Firecracker Leadership Framework indicators using a scale of 1 (low) to 5 (high). You can download a copy of the table from www.suemusson.com. Total your score for each of the three areas: head, hands, heart. This will help you identify whether your leadership is in balance and whether there are any areas for you to prioritise in your own development.

Choose no more than three skills to address initially. Select one skill that represents a significant gap for you and one skill that you enjoy the most. The former gives you an opportunity to improve, the latter reinforces the pleasure you gain by continuing to grow in an area that is already a strength.

The final column of the table highlights the chapters of this book that address specific indicators. This will help you home in on the content you might find of most relevance to your development priorities right now.

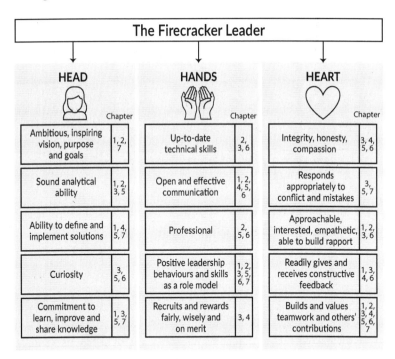

The Firecracker Leader

HEAD	Chapter	HANDS	Chapter	HEART	Chapter
Ambitious, inspiring vision, purpose and goals	1, 2, 7	Up-to-date technical skills	2, 3, 6	Integrity, honesty, compassion	3, 4, 5, 6
Sound analytical ability	1, 2, 3, 5	Open and effective communication	1, 2, 4, 5, 6	Responds appropriately to conflict and mistakes	3, 5, 7
Ability to define and implement solutions	1, 4, 5, 7	Professional	2, 5, 6	Approachable, interested, empathetic, able to build rapport	1, 2, 3, 6
Curiosity	3, 5, 6	Positive leadership behaviours and skills as a role model	1, 2, 3, 5, 6, 7	Readily gives and receives constructive feedback	1, 3, 4, 6
Commitment to learn, improve and share knowledge	1, 3, 5, 7	Recruits and rewards fairly, wisely and on merit	3, 4	Builds and values teamwork and others' contributions	1, 2, 3, 4, 5, 6, 7

ONE
How To Inspire Others

'If your actions inspire others to dream more, learn more, do more and become more, you are a leader.'
attributed to John Quincy Adams

I t is easy to miss the significance of these words. I know because when this quote was first sent to me, I glanced at it and dismissed it. This is nothing more than a saying on a fridge magnet, I thought.

Sometime later, when I was asked to give a lecture to a group of Masters' students on leadership, I came across this quote again. I read it properly, and it struck me as the most perfect definition of leadership. Over the years, I have started countless presentations on leadership with reference to this insightful quote.

It appears deceptively simple, but it is profound. Leadership, in a nutshell, is all about three things: prioritising others, being a good role model and having a positive impact.

Are you a leader according to this definition? Who is following you? Have your actions inspired others to dream, learn, do and become more?

In this chapter, I want to share the key to inspiring others and the practical tools you can use to master this fundamental aspect of leadership.

Inspiration – anyone can do it

Leadership has absolutely nothing to do with a job title, organisational structure, pay or status. People who equate being a manager with being a leader miss the point. Leadership is not about your seniority, the number of people who report to you, or where you park your car.

Your position may command some respect, but a job title alone will never be truly inspirational to others. It is your actions in a role that make the difference.

Leaders who inspire, follow a pattern of behaviour that anyone can replicate. First and foremost, they have a clear **rationale** for their actions. This is derived from their ability to analyse information to determine what is needed and why.

Second, they connect this analysis to an ambitious **purpose** that they and others find meaningful.

Third, they explain and **communicate** this information in a way that makes it relevant, inclusive and motivational to others. They connect the purpose and goals of the team in such a way that followers feel motivated to action themselves, including seeking to improve their own knowledge and skills to make a bigger contribution.

Finally, the inspirational leader notices the efforts of others and takes every opportunity to praise and **recognise** the difference others make.

Inspiration creates a virtuous cycle, unlocking more discretionary effort from followers who dream, learn, do and become more. Sounds simple, so why do so many leaders struggle to do this effectively in practice?

There are four main reasons:

- **Analysis gap** – a failure to analyse data to develop meaningful purpose and goals

- **Communication gap** – a failure to articulate purpose and goals in a relevant, inclusive way that motivates others

- **Humility gap** – a failure to be others-driven because of ego; this is the look-at-me leader

- **Confidence gap** – a failure to be others-driven because of a lack of confidence; this is the imposter syndrome leader

Any one of these gaps will derail your efforts to inspire others, but all of them can be overcome. It just takes insight and commitment to improve.

Overcoming the analysis gap

The inspirational leader is always curious and eager to understand current reality. They gather information, they are observational and they ask 'why' questions. They are good listeners.

Having established data, they spend time analysing and reflecting on this information. This process is the foundation for being able to articulate purpose, solve problems and set meaningful improvement goals in a way that is motivational to others.

CASE STUDY: It was definitely not all about car parking

When I took on my first chair role, I arranged a handover with my predecessor who had served for nearly a decade in the role. I was taken aback when he told me we would not need to talk for long – he believed there really was not much to cover as everything was under control.

He then asked if I wanted to know the biggest problem I would face. Yes, I answered, sitting with pen poised.

'Car parking,' was his reply.

I thought for a moment he was joking, especially as I was well aware of the numerous challenges the organisation faced. In preparing my application, I had read past board papers, observed a board meeting and held introductory meetings with executive and non-executive directors. It was clear the organisation had significant financial, operational and governance problems, so I was immensely surprised that my predecessor seemed to possess such a massive analysis gap.

Any pretence that things were fine and under control was dispelled within a few weeks of my arrival when I received three separate whistleblowings alleging serious misconduct by senior individuals. These allegations of misconduct spanned a range of breaches and certainly did not include car parking.

To deal appropriately with this situation, it was necessary to commission an independent investigation into all the allegations so that evidence could be gathered and fair decisions made. Several members of the executive team were suspended while investigation and disciplinary processes were underway. The evidence that emerged confirmed this was a troubled and poorly led organisation. In the end, the chief executive was dismissed for gross misconduct, and one other director resigned and would have been dismissed had she stayed in post.

This example is an extreme reminder of what can happen if wilful blindness and denial are combined with a significant analysis gap.

Over the last decade, I have chaired three large National Health Service (NHS) trusts, working with nine different chief executives. The best of these leaders demonstrated open minds and analytical skills in abundance. They were like sponges, seeking and absorbing complex information. They were quick to ask questions and show interest, looking far and wide. Additionally, they were able to evaluate information at speed. The best were also masterful in sharing their analysis with board colleagues, often bringing well-reasoned proposals where they were careful to show their workings, sharing the thought process they had applied to develop their ideas.

Be honest with yourself and consider whether your analytical skills are up to scratch. Here are some suggestions if you feel your analytical skills could be better:

- Commit to reading more to train your brain. Reading helps you process data more effectively and improves your ability to find solutions. It creates the right mental space to support insight and intuition. The list in the 'Further Reading' section includes relevant books for developing analytical and problem-solving skills.

- Set more time for observation, ask good questions, listen carefully and write down what you learn.

- Ask 'why?' at least five times in relation to a problem to strengthen your ability to identify root causes. This is also an opportunity to convey curiosity and interest to others.

- Triangulate, order and evaluate all the data you have gathered. Know that synthesising this information will trigger the creative process of finding solutions.

- Test potential solutions and discuss them with others.

- Use forecasting and modelling to connect solutions to purpose and goals.

Overcoming the communication gap

Not every leader is a born public speaker, but every inspirational leader has mastered the ability to articulate their analysis in such a way that their audience feels informed, included and motivated.

Inspirational communication means painting a compelling picture of a future state that helps the listener share in that future state, identify what contribution they can make and become motivated to act. The first building block is having the right content. If you have developed an ambitious purpose and clear goals based on robust analysis, you are halfway there.

The delivery of the message is just as important as the content. A skilful communicator will personalise the content, particularly through storytelling, so that followers not only understand the relevance of the goals, but also connect to them, creating a sense of ownership and commitment to do their part.

Assess your ability to frame purpose and goals and to deliver your analysis in an inclusive and motivational way. Be honest with yourself, taking into account any feedback you have received.

Chances are, you may be one of the 75% of the population whose biggest fear is public speaking.[2] Again, through insight and a commitment to change, you can overcome this fear and develop the confidence to communicate inspirationally.

CASE STUDY - Fifteen minutes of agony

Today, I am a confident communicator who thoroughly enjoys public speaking, but it was not always so. Early in my career, I was responsible for organising a national conference on economic development. My job was to brief the speakers and oversee all aspects of the content for the conference, making sure each session contained meaningful information of practical use to the delegates.

On the eve of the conference, one of the speakers pulled out, and my boss decided that I should step in and deliver the speech. I reluctantly agreed on the basis that the speech was already written and the notes would be sent over to me.

Unfortunately, the promised 'notes' arrived on the day and contained only the bullet points I myself had sent to the scheduled speaker as a guide to the content he should prepare. He had added nothing.

It was the stuff of nightmares. I suddenly found myself in front of an audience of several hundred delegates with no content and no personal knowledge of the subject area. I can still recall the horrendous physical sensations: dry mouth, racing heart, stomach turning somersaults, rising flush covering my neck and face. I felt uncomfortable, embarrassed, out of my depth. My voice was strained and breathless as I somehow managed to stumble through fifteen minutes of agony.

It was really quite traumatising, but this awful experience also gave me the determination I needed to make sure I was never, ever in that position again.

The most painful experience can serve as the most effective catalyst for personal growth. I went on to train myself to become a confident, inspirational public speaker. I learned through personal experience that there are ten practical steps to overcoming the communication gap.

Head: Your brainpower

1. Preparation

Prepare your material. Do your research. Know your facts. Know your audience and their interests. Refine your content. Make sure your analysis is sound and your message is compelling and relevant to your audience.

Personally, I like to type out my presentations, and then rehearse them out loud in front of a mirror to hear the cadence and tone of the words. Using this approach allows me to test and refine the content so that I feel confident it is fit for purpose.

2. Storytelling

The best presentations involve telling stories. This helps your audience identify with the content, enabling them to enter the scenario you are describing. Their recall of your message is also enhanced through storytelling. Your audience will remember the story you tell, but they will rarely remember more than one point you say or put on a slide.

3. Visual aids

Too many people produce wordy, boring slides, and then read the words on the slides verbatim to their audience. This dreadful practice is aptly known as 'death by PowerPoint'.

Most people think in pictures. If you are using slides, make sure they are visually appealing. Slides that contain an appealing image are more likely to be recalled by your audience. Clear images that connect the audience to your words are the most effective visual aids. If your slides do contain words, be succinct and include no more than a few bullet points.

Hands: Your technical skill

4. Practise, practise, practise

You need to practise the delivery of your material until it feels natural and effortless to give your talk using a conversational style. Test through rehearsal that you are using the correct pace, energy and tone for maximum effect.

5. Rehearse in front of a mirror

Looking at yourself in the mirror while you practise has so many benefits. Crucially, this approach allows you to see the 70% of your communication that is non-verbal.[3] By looking in the mirror, you are able to see what your audience sees: your facial expressions, your hand gestures and the way you hold yourself.

6. Use affirmations

Looking in the mirror enhances the power of using affirmations to lock in the outcome you want. You might say, 'My message is inspiring for every member of my audience' or 'I am a confident communicator who loves public speaking' or 'This is the best speech I have ever given'.

These affirmations spoken aloud to your reflection in the mirror convince your subconscious mind that the statements are true. This makes it unsurprising and natural when the delivery of your talk matches the words in your affirmations.

Most importantly, using positive affirmations is the best way to counter the impact of negative self-talk. Leaders who are fearful of public speaking often subject themselves to discouraging comments in their own heads that undermine their confidence and ability to inspire others. What you expect and believe will happen – for good or ill – is what you will come to experience.

7. Rehearse with a mental video

Another powerful rehearsal technique is to close your eyes and play a mental video of what you will feel, see and hear as you deliver your talk.

Feel how calm and confident you are in front of your audience. Feel how much you are enjoying sharing your message. See the response you desire from the audience. Seeing every member of your audience listening attentively, nodding, smiling and connecting to your content in your mind's eye is the best way to programme that outcome in reality. Hear your own voice with the right tone and pace to captivate your audience.

Every time you play this mental video, you are training your subconscious to deliver the result you desire.

8. Practise with someone you trust

If you have a trusted colleague or friend who will listen to your talk and give you encouragement and constructive feedback, you can test out the content and your delivery with them as part of your preparation.

 Heart: Your ability to care with love and compassion

9. Invite your listeners into your story

Personalise the content and make sure it is meaningful for others. Think about who is in the audience and what they most want from your talk. Tell stories that add emotion and feeling to your content. This invites your audience to enter the scenario you are describing.

If you personalise the content and add emotion and feeling, your audience will connect to your message. This will help them relate to you and will make the content you share more memorable for them.

10. Create memorable moments and lasting impact

Sometimes you will not get an immediate sense of how your message has landed with your audience. Do not be alarmed if you do not see a response straight away. When you get this right, your content will go beyond getting a laugh or a nod and will stay with others in a deeper, more lasting way.

On many occasions, I have had individuals mention how a story I told or an experience I shared stayed with them and what it meant to them – sometimes months or years after the event. I take that as the greatest compliment I can receive. It is so rewarding to share something others find meaningful, helpful and motivational.

If you can imagine yourself loving public speaking, feeling the happiness that comes with doing something well that benefits others, you will train your subconscious mind to create this outcome in reality. To paraphrase Napoleon Hill, as with all goals, you need to believe the outcome you desire can be achieved.[4] If you believe the outcome has already been achieved through affirmation and visualisation, your mind will deliver that result for you.

There are plenty of books you can read and courses you can take to improve your communication skills, and you should never believe that you have finished growing in this crucial area. Even if you feel you are a confident and accomplished public speaker, there is always something new to learn by reading more and participating in more training. You will find plenty of relevant resources in the 'Further Reading' section.

Overcoming the humility gap

This section could have been titled 'The awfulness of the look-at-me leader'. These leaders struggle to inspire others because they are ego or self-driven.

They are so focused on themselves, they never really give much thought to anyone else.

Ego-driven leaders simply cannot stop telling you how great they are. They also have an exhausting tendency to ask you to validate their greatness. Some people confuse this absence of humility with being confident. The inverse is actually much more likely to be true. The look-at-me leader has a whiny need to be told they are amazing usually because they lack confidence and self-belief.

The root cause of the look-at-me leader has been described as a failure to develop an inner sense of worth or self-esteem such that the individual is entirely dependent on receiving admiration from others.[5] Perhaps the most extreme example of the humility gap is Donald Trump. Countless articles have been written about his all-consuming obsession with his own merits, his constant refrain of grandiosity, describing himself as the best and as being perfect at everything, and his victim mentality. His particular brand of ego has been diagnosed as narcissistic personality disorder by psychologists and former colleagues.[6, 7]

I have encountered a less extreme version of the look-at-me leader many times. One such occasion involved a visit from a senior government minister to the NHS trust I was chairing.

CASE STUDY – Praise where praise is not due

The collapse of a construction firm led to the discovery of hundreds of serious structural defects that rendered a new hospital building dangerously unsafe, delaying its opening by five years.

Although the building looked finished, the internal defects were so significant that it was necessary to implement an incredibly complex remediation programme. This involved techniques that had never been used before, such as bonding new concrete to existing concrete and adding steelwork to the frame of a large hospital infrastructure. All this activity took place in the midst of a global pandemic, which added significant risk and operational challenge to an already complex process.

The team involved successfully oversaw the repair programme and the safe move into the new hospital. They completed an immensely technical challenge on time and on budget, did an amazing job and deserve great praise for their professionalism, resilience and commitment.

At a small celebration event, as the chair of the organisation, I thanked the team for their incredible dedication and said, 'Remember that success has many fathers. There will be an endless stream of people claiming credit for what you have achieved. Let them get on. We know what we know.'

This proved prophetic. On the government minister's arrival, as soon as he had got out of the car and posed for the cameras, sure enough, he informed me that he had been personally responsible for making the new hospital happen. The fact that he had had zero involvement over the five years that the hospital team dealt with the massive consequences of the building firm's collapse was immaterial in his narrative that cast him as the hero. During his visit, he expressed no interest in the repair programme and no gratitude for the tireless efforts of those who had actually enabled the safe and successful occupation of the new building.

Later in his visit, he had arranged to meet with trade union leaders and a cross-section of staff. After these meetings concluded, he strode over to me with a look of smug satisfaction and said, 'Well, that's told them. You should never assume. I told them my father was a trade unionist.'

It escaped me what precise relevance that fact had to anything or why it was meant to impress me. I did feel like responding, 'My dad was a surgeon. Does that mean you would be happy for me to remove your appendix?'

The look-at-me leader never succeeds in inspiring others to dream, learn, do and become more because they simply cannot see beyond themselves. They are incapable of moving beyond their need for attention and adulation to be driven by genuine concern for others.

The answer in film

I love sports films. They follow a fantastic formula: the underdogs triumph over adversity by building character, practising hard and earning their success. Often their coach or leader provides the analysis and inspiration that enables the team to reverse their fortunes and begin winning.

The formula of dream, struggle, victory in sports movies illustrates my Firecracker Leadership philosophy. Quite simply, to triumph, a team has to understand what they have to do differently to win; put in the effort by practising and performing; and commit wholly to the endeavour.

They need inspiration (head), perspiration (hands) and dedication (heart) in abundance and in balance to triumph.

One film stands out in demonstrating brilliantly how the look-at-me leader is such a liability. *Coach Carter* is based on a true story, recounting the return of a former star player to coach a high school basketball team in a deprived California community.[8] Coach Carter inspires his players to learn that character, courtesy, discipline, effort and team work deliver success.

As the film progresses, the team builds a small winning streak. At that point, several egos start to get out of control with players strutting around, crowing about their prowess and diminishing their opponents.

In the next practice, as the players are running various drills, every time there is a basket, Coach Carter exclaims, 'That's me, baby. I did that. All day, baby, all day. I did that.'[9] The players are a bit confused, but carry on regardless.

Coach Carter bends down to tie his shoe and shouts, 'Look at that bow. I tied that. I tied that! Who wants to give me some?' As one of the players moves to high-five him, Coach Carter shouts, 'No! What is wrong with you?'

He tells the team they are acting like punks, swaggering with a self-congratulatory strut and seeking applause. He tells them they have no right to behave this way and instead need to 'Show some class. Act like a champion.'

That is such a great illustration of my point. Inspirational leaders do not need to remind you incessantly how great they are. They don't need to preen and big themselves up while knocking others down. Great leaders quietly know what they know. They are 'classy champions', in Coach Carter's parlance. They let their actions do the talking and focus on serving the team.

The agreeable look-at-me leader

There is another type of look-at-me leader. On the face of it, they are much more agreeable and less self-aggrandising, but just as insecure and needy as their brasher counterparts. This more subtle version of the look-at-me leader tends to repeat a triumphal event or a third-party endorsement – all so they can steer the conversation to gaining your agreement that they are indeed wonderful.

I worked with a colleague who constantly referred to an occasion when she gave permission for a team to recruit a temporary project manager to help with an operational challenge. Every time she told this story – which she did frequently – her tale would always end with the team nearly weeping with gratitude, telling her that she was amazing and thanking her for stepping in to fix all their problems.

She would pause at that point, waiting for an approving chorus of endorsement. If sufficient praise was not offered straight away, she would ask, 'What do you think of that?'

I would usually give an anodyne response like, 'It sounds as if you were really helpful, and the team appreciated your support.' This would trigger a quest for more compliments, such as, 'Oh, do you really think so? Do you think my intervention made all that difference? I was just doing my job, but it's nice to know that you feel I did this so well. Yes, they really did need my help.' It was almost as if she had convinced herself that I had spontaneously brought up her leadership triumph and not that she had contrived a situation to extract a compliment.

I had another colleague who would start a conversation with a long list of his personal qualities and finish with something like, 'I'm a reflective person. As a leader, I'm totally committed to personal development. I have great insight. I know my strengths so I'm comfortable with feedback. You should feel free to give me feedback.' Although this sounded like a genuine request, what I learned was that he really did not want feedback. He wanted approval and endorsement that he possessed the strengths he had described.

To be fair, both of these colleagues were in no way awful people, and they did have strengths, but their constant need for validation seriously compromised their impact as credible leaders. Instead of feeling inspired, colleagues found the repetition of their search for praise wearing and tiresome.

If you have got this far in this book, I doubt that you are a look-at-me leader! Nonetheless, it is worth reflecting on whether you are role modelling the classy champion behaviours that represent being others-driven. Perhaps you experience occasional feelings of insecurity that distract you from being as focused on others as you wish to be.

Think back over the last week or two and consider if, in your interactions with others, you fell into the humility gap. If so, you have identified a valid improvement area. Awareness is the first step to minimising or banishing the negative behaviours that can undermine your leadership impact.

To address the humility gap:

- Avoid talking about yourself. Be the classy champion Coach Carter respects.

- Use affirmations that remind you that you are a confident leader who is committed to serving others. While you appreciate positive feedback, you have no need to pressure others to give you adulation.

- If you slip into talking about yourself, remind yourself to ask questions instead. This shifts your focus outwards and demonstrates sincere interest in others.

- Think about your colleagues. Ask and reflect on what they need, how you can best recognise their achievements, how you can provide support and be of service to them. Share your observations with them to test whether they share your analysis.

- Read more about working in teams and supporting others. You will find some suggestions for relevant reading material in the 'Further Reading' section.

- Resolve never to fish for compliments! Instead, gather meaningful feedback on your leadership in a structured, professional way (see Chapter 6).

Overcoming the confidence gap

A recent study by KPMG found that 75% of the 750 female executive leaders surveyed suffered from imposter syndrome.[10] Imposter syndrome sufferers experience a debilitating lack of self-confidence. They compare themselves unfavourably to others, and they feel inadequate, anxious, overwhelmed by unachievable expectations and crippled by self-doubt and negative self-talk. They feel unworthy of success.

Of the women leaders surveyed in that study, a whopping 85% believed imposter syndrome is experienced by women at work. About 75% felt that men do not experience the same feelings of self-doubt as frequently. These findings are really depressing, but not surprising. At these levels of prevalence, it is clear that the confidence gap is a significant barrier for women leaders.

I was recently included in an email chain of female leaders discussing their interest in personal development. It was heartbreaking to learn that so many accomplished, talented, skilled, intelligent, compassionate women were suffering from feelings of anxiety and doubt about their own abilities. These were mainly highly qualified, experienced doctors and nurses, many at the peak of their profession, working in the health sector.

I feel dismayed by the frequency and severity of the confidence gap occurring for women leaders. How can it be that so many capable women find themselves sabotaged unnecessarily by these feelings of inadequacy?

Too many women seem to have absorbed a belief that it is wrong for them to be confident and that expressing self-confidence is somehow unseemly or a manifestation of ego or arrogance. That simply is not true. Self-confidence is a wonderful trait. It is appealing and positive and inspires others.

There is absolutely nothing wrong with feeling confident and appreciative of your abilities and strengths. You just have to be a classy champion and walk with a quiet inner belief. It is this kind of self-confidence that others find magnetic and inspirational.

It is frustrating that so many women confess to suffering from imposter syndrome, and then stop at that. It's almost as if in owning that label, they have agreed to live within the limitations of imposter syndrome forever. Don't get me wrong. I know imposter syndrome is real and that it takes courage to admit to being a sufferer, but you have to be willing to move beyond the diagnosis. If you go no further than declaring, 'I suffer with imposter syndrome', you are undermining your own ability to develop the confidence and self-belief you need to fulfil your leadership potential.

You do need to be honest with yourself about whether your skills are in balance. Remember, you can score your skills using the framework in the introduction. Most impostor syndrome sufferers have a surfeit of heart qualities. They are often people pleasers who want to be liked and avoid conflict. This imbalance causes inner turmoil and reinforces the imposter's feelings of inadequacy.

The confidence gap and imposter syndrome do not have to be permanent features. They can be overcome if you choose to do so. Recognising you suffer from imposter syndrome is the first step to eradicating it.

In the KPMG study, the respondents highlighted three things that helped reduce negative feelings associated with imposter syndrome.[11] These were:

- Having a supportive manager.

- Feeling valued and rewarded.

- Accessing advice from a mentor or trusted advisor when taking on a new role.

These are external inputs. As a leader, you may want to consider if this kind of support is available for you and your female colleagues.

There are also positive actions that every individual can take personally to build self-confidence and overcome the feelings of inadequacy that characterise imposter syndrome. These include:

- Use positive affirmations to change your self-talk. You might repeat something like, 'I used to suffer with imposter syndrome, and now I have an abundance of self-confidence that helps me inspire others.'

- Practise gratitude for your positive skills and abilities. Recognise and appreciate what you are good at. This will give you inner confidence and belief.

- Seek and review feedback (see Chapter 6) to help you identify a better understanding of your strengths and how these benefit others. This will build a solid foundation for your self-belief.

Summary

This chapter has described how inspiration comes from being others-driven, not ego-driven. The ability to inspire others is not connected to a job title or status. It is a by-product of your skill as a leader to analyse information, set an ambitious purpose and goals, articulate your vision in a motivational and inclusive way, and recognise the contributions that others make.

There are four gaps that undermine your ability to inspire others. These are:

- The analysis gap

- The communication gap

- The humility gap

- The confidence gap

All of these can be overcome through insight and a willingness to take action. The chapter provides practical steps you can take to become an inspiring leader.

The Firecracker Leader	The Poor Leader
• Inspires others to dream, learn, do and become more • Sets clear direction • Is others-driven • Communicates confidently	• Fails to articulate a clear purpose • Is ego-driven, craving attention and praise • Fears public speaking • Wears the mantle of imposter syndrome

This chapter has covered the following Firecracker Leadership Framework attributes:

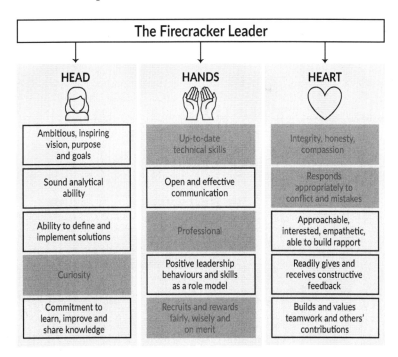

The Firecracker Leader

HEAD	HANDS	HEART
Ambitious, inspiring vision, purpose and goals	Up-to-date technical skills	Integrity, honesty, compassion
Sound analytical ability	Open and effective communication	Responds appropriately to conflict and mistakes
Ability to define and implement solutions	Professional	Approachable, interested, empathetic, able to build rapport
Curiosity	Positive leadership behaviours and skills as a role model	Readily gives and receives constructive feedback
Commitment to learn, improve and share knowledge	Recruits and rewards fairly, wisely and on merit	Builds and values teamwork and others' contributions

TWO

How To Set Purpose

The key task of a leader is to articulate purpose and ambition in a way that speaks effectively to others, building commitment, motivation and action.

Every individual you lead needs to feel included and be crystal clear on their contribution to achieving the purpose and goals that have been set. The purpose you choose must be big. Only something significant and worthy will ignite the commitment of others.

A lofty, stretching, ambitious purpose acts as a magnet, attracting talented people who strive to attain the purpose and goals. People with the best brains and abilities want to be part of big and meaningful endeavours.

Imagine what it would be like to lead a team fuelled by an electrifying purpose with all members sharing common goals. This chapter gives examples of how to set a motivational purpose that inspires others to action. It also describes five common pitfalls to avoid.

St Jude Children's Research Hospital

The best example I have ever seen of setting meaningful purpose and goals is St Jude Children's Research Hospital in Memphis, Tennessee.

This is an organisation that knows its purpose through and through. When you visit, every member of staff you encounter asks if you are aware of the founder's vision and the story behind the hospital's creation.

It's a great story.

St Jude was founded by US entertainer Danny Thomas in 1962 in gratitude for his personal success. Danny Thomas, a devout Catholic and aspiring entertainer, prayed to St Jude – the patron saint of lost causes – for a career breakthrough. He promised that if he became a success, he would build a shrine to the saint.

Soon after, he got his big break in television and made good on his promise. The shrine he built was to become St Jude Children's Research Hospital.

Danny Thomas established the hospital with a clear purpose: that no child should die at the dawn of life. St Jude would address the most serious, seemingly incurable childhood illnesses, such as acute lymphoblastic leukaemia (ALL) which had just a 4% survival rate at the time the hospital was founded.

Using the founder's vision as the filter to set goals and invest in scientific discovery, research, treatment and care, St Jude has achieved remarkable success. Today, the ALL survival rate is 94%. The overall survival rate of all childhood cancers has increased from 20% in 1962 to 80% today.[12]

St Jude is a centre of international research and clinical excellence boasting Nobel Prize winning staff within its ranks. The ambitious purpose of the organisation attracts the highest calibre people. The hospital regularly features as one of the USA's best employers with exceptional staff satisfaction levels and low workforce turnover.

The level of pride that staff feel in the organisation's success is palpable. Each individual – whether a clinician, researcher, support worker or volunteer – will talk unprompted about the hospital's purpose and their role in making the founder's vision a reality. Danny Thomas used his fame to host fundraising events in partnership with local business leaders. This approach created a powerful charitable funding model that generated the funds necessary for the hospital to fulfil its purpose.

The hospital receives hundreds of millions of dollars each year in charitable donations from individuals and corporations. These resources are used to support research and to provide care to children experiencing the most serious illnesses. Charitable donations also enable St Jude to make good on the founder's commitment to treat all children in need, regardless of the ability to pay.

These impressive achievements started with a big, meaningful, ambitious purpose that ignited belief and effort at scale. The founder's purpose has endured for over sixty years.

Finding life-saving treatments for sick children is a purpose that speaks to humans on a profound level. This purpose not only galvanises the work of thousands of hospital employees every day, it also unlocks generous support from individual and corporate donors nationwide.

I found my visit to St Jude inspiring and so instructive in helping me understand how powerful it is when a leader articulates a truly meaningful purpose – one that connects to people deeply, guides decision making and aligns behaviours, priorities, operational action and results.

Inspiration blockers

Every leader has the opportunity to set a purpose that stirs the spirit and transcends the mundane, but there are lots of reasons why this can be challenging to do in practice. There are five pitfalls to avoid when setting purpose.

1. Lack of imagination

This is a failure to think big enough. Often, fear or being consumed by here-and-now pressures is at the root of this. Many leaders benefit from working with a coach or mentor to expand their vision. Spending more time reading and conversing with people you find inspirational are also good remedies.

2. The current reality trap

This is aiming low in the guise of being realistic. It sounds plausible, but it is really just a manifestation of a lack of courage when the purpose is bound too closely to the comfort zone of current reality. A purpose that represents what is being done now plus a bit more will not fire the imagination of anyone.

Imagine if Danny Thomas had replaced the purpose of St Jude – 'no child should die in the dawn of life' – with 'survival rates for children with ALL should double'. This would aim to increase survival rates from 4% to 8%, a world away from the 94% survival rate that his ambitious vision has actually produced.

The realistic purpose rarely inspires or endures because it is too limited and too close to status quo. A meaningful purpose needs to be big and just a little scary to contemplate. If it is too prosaic and close to current reality, it will not unlock motivation, creativity and effort in its pursuit.

3. Conflicting or too many priorities and targets

Defining one purpose and no more than three priorities at a time gives you the best chance of helping others connect and commit to their pursuit. Making sure your three priorities have a clear rationale and a logical alignment to the purpose is essential.

This is easier said than done, particularly in highly regulated sectors at the mercy of political tinkering, such as healthcare or education. Organisations in these sectors face a baffling array of conflicting priorities and targets. For example, NHS organisations in the UK are exhorted to reduce waiting lists, increase productivity, meet quality targets, speed up ambulance handovers, improve staffing ratios and staff retention, research new treatments, reduce patients' length of stay, do more elective activity, discharge patients more quickly, stop spending on agency and temporary staffing, invest in digital technology, get upstream and prevent illness, work collaboratively with partners, address health inequalities and make significant savings – all at the same time. It is easy to lose focus when surrounded by so many frequently changing instructions.

It takes courage and a clear head to avoid passing on a muddle of conflicting priorities as though they make sense. Effective leaders rise above the fray and articulate a single unifying purpose and a logical number of priorities to preserve organisational clarity and effort.

4. Overwhelm

The flip side of setting a big, ambitious purpose is that it can be daunting, leaving people overwhelmed and feeling beaten before they start. An effective leader will keep the purpose in frame while taking care to set out the baby steps that can be taken to make progress towards achieving the purpose.

No ambitious purpose will ever be achieved overnight. It is important to set out what can be done today, and then to articulate how this contributes to the achievement of the purpose. Taking a frequent look back to track and celebrate progress along the way will help to sustain motivation and effort.

Great leaders can combat overwhelm by making the link between purpose, goals and individual contributions crystal clear. This process makes individuals feel included and part of a team that is aiming high and working hard in pursuit of milestones or goals along the way to achieving a big purpose.

When I spoke to a volunteer at St Jude's, she explained how spending time playing with children while they were inpatients was contributing to their recovery. She worked with clinical staff as a member of the team to schedule play as part of every patient's treatment plan. She articulated how her volunteering was helping to achieve the founder's vision, one patient at a time.

5. Making it about you

A meaningful purpose appeals to others because it strikes an emotional chord and has relevance to them. St Jude's purpose has a universality of appeal because it is about saving sick children's lives. Pretty much everyone I have ever met can relate to the merit of that endeavour.

One sure-fire way to kill off other people's motivation and enthusiasm is to articulate a purpose that is all about you, your status and your success. It is off-putting to be asked to work in pursuit of one individual's personal gain.

I experienced this when a new regulatory body was created to oversee NHS activity in my region. The new chairman came to see me when he took up his appointment. At this first meeting, he spent a lot of time telling me that his success was dependent on my organisation's performance, so this needed to be my top priority. I found this really repulsive. Needless to say, my organisation's purpose was focused on meeting the local population's healthcare needs, not securing his personal success. Yuck.

Making sense of complexity

A great leader will make sense of complexity to set a meaningful purpose. This often requires the ability to clarify and simplify without dumbing down, and it can take courage and determination to stick with what you know to be right.

CASE STUDY – The magic number

Several years ago when I was a non-executive director of a children's hospital, I was asked to work with a team to prepare for a national review of paediatric cardiac surgery. The purpose of the review was to establish the optimal number and location of surgery centres across the country to deliver safe and sustainable services. It was clear that the panel would recommend reducing the number of centres, thereby creating winners and losers.

The review was conducted by an independent expert panel which visited every centre to score its capability against a number of standards. Two areas were weighted in the assessment: activity and leadership vision.

In preparing for the panel's visit, our local team gathered and analysed population health statistics, performance data, financial results, staffing information and qualitative information, including clinical outcomes and parent feedback, to produce an evidence-based self-assessment against all the quality standards. We met several times to make sure everyone involved was comfortable with the analysis and had up-to-date knowledge of the service.

Once we reached a point of shared understanding, the lead surgeon articulated the purpose of our centre. He described his many years of training in centres of excellence around the world. This activity had developed his competence to perform open heart surgery on neonates of zero to two days old whose hearts were the size of a walnut. I was utterly blown away by his ability to state something so complex, technical and frankly frightening in such a clear and compassionate way.

He said, 'All of this means surgeons must complete 300 surgeries per year. You have seen the incidence of heart disease among neonates and children in the catchment area. There is another reason that I have discussed with my mentors. If the number is 299, then my surgical skills are not practised enough to be at peak level. I need to do 300 to perform at my best. There is also a good reason why the number is not 301. If I do 301 surgeries, that is too many for me to know the first name of every patient's parents and grandparents.'

What a great demonstration of setting purpose incorporating head, hands and heart. He described the analysis of health statistics and data (head). He linked this to maintaining up-to-date expert technical skills (literally, hands). He made knowing the first names of worried parents and grandparents a priority (heart) so that he could provide compassionate care and reassurance to them at such a stressful time.

Purpose outside healthcare

Although the two examples I have shared so far in the chapter describe how to set purpose in the world of paediatric medicine, they do represent good practice that is applicable to any environment and sector.

Many years ago, I was working as a management consultant. The government had established training and enterprise councils (TECs) as independent organisations to oversee vocational training for young people and to provide business advice to local employers. The company I worked for assisted TECs throughout the country to conduct market assessments to enable them to define their purpose and offer relevant services.

I was struck by how similar and pedestrian the mission statements and business plans were of all but one of the TECs. One stood out because the chief executive of that organisation was truly a visionary leader. Where his contemporaries talked of implementing government schemes and policies in the same way as usual, he articulated the organisation's purpose as sparking aspiration, achievement and social justice for young people.

The staff were inspired by this purpose, and the organisation's goals were clearly aligned to its achievement. The staff worked with notable energy, creativity and commitment. They set up new systems; they tried innovative approaches; and they engaged directly with employers, young people and families to develop personalised programmes for achieving vocational qualifications, apprenticeships and skilled jobs. They created groupings or cohorts of young people to engender a sense of connection and organised celebration events to recognise each group's achievements.

The staff spoke with appreciation, respect and loyalty when they referred to their visionary leader. There was a palpable buzz when you walked through the door, confirming that this was an organisation with a clear sense of purpose and a motivated workforce.

The other TECs seemed to lack this oomph. Walking into their offices was much like walking into the regional outpost of any government agency: quiet, low key, process-driven and a world away from inspirational.

Summary

This chapter has described how great leaders set an ambitious, meaningful purpose. It has given examples of good practice in this process and shared five common blockers that can undermine the setting of a meaningful purpose:

- Lack of imagination

- The current reality trap

- Conflicting or too many priorities and targets

- Overwhelm

- Making it about you

All of these can be avoided or overcome by thinking big, making an emotional connection and identifying appropriate milestones. Identifying a purpose whose achievement will be of benefit to others is crucial to creating energy, effort and commitment.

The Firecracker Leader	The Poor Leader
• Thinks big • Applies head, hands, heart in setting one purpose and no more than three aligned priorities • Connects the purpose to milestones and individual contributions so that others understand their role and the difference they make • Focuses effort and energy on a purpose that benefits others	• Constrains ambition in favour of being realistic • Sacrifices a clear purpose to external demands and here-and-now pressures • Prioritises too many goals • Lacks courage in clarifying and setting a clear purpose that benefits others • Sets a self-aggrandising purpose

This chapter has covered the following Firecracker Leadership Framework attributes:

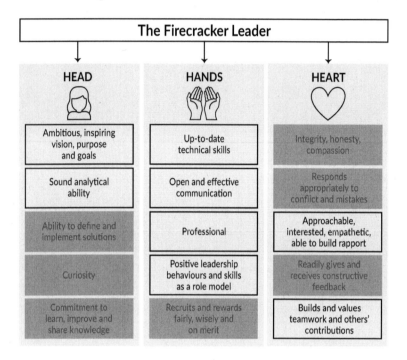

THREE

How To Build
A Winning Team

Leadership is a team sport. Having personal competence is a great asset, but if you cannot build and
motivate a team to work well together, your impact as
a leader will always be limited. The team you build is
all important in achieving your purpose.

Great leaders recognise they do not have to be personally brilliant at everything. Instead, they concentrate
their talent on understanding the whole chessboard of
skill requirements so they can recruit and motivate the
best possible team of experts to cover all the squares.

Confident leaders aspire to work with people who are
much better than they are in key areas of competence.
Insecure leaders do the opposite. They seek to avoid
feeling threatened or challenged at all costs.

Weak leaders tend to recruit people who enable them to stay in a comfort zone. This means, when given the choice, they will appoint a mini-me, someone with a similar skill profile to their own, but at a more junior level. Weak leaders avoid confronting their own shortcomings by steering clear of people who are different to them and possess star quality. They find these qualities too threatening.

Leading the process of building a winning team requires competence in six areas:

- **Strategic analysis**: This is the ability to assess the whole chessboard of current and future skill requirements to set clear role profiles and expectations of team members.

- **Selling vacancies**: This is the ability to articulate roles in an appealing way to attract the most capable applicants who represent a diversity of knowledge, skill and background.

- **Recruiting with integrity**: This means using recruitment processes that are fair and merit-based.

- **Welcoming and integrating**: This means effective on-boarding arrangements are in place to support newcomers in starting and fitting in.

- **Retaining**: This means having in place the right processes for remuneration, review, team building, talent management, succession and development.

- **Taking action when it all goes wrong**: This means grasping the nettle of poor performance or unacceptable behaviours quickly and appropriately to avoid their toxic consequences.

This chapter describes good practice and poor practice in the five competence areas involved in building a winning team. Because recruitment decisions are so crucial, this chapter is longer and more detailed than others in this book.

Analysing the skill chessboard

As described in Chapter 1, great leaders possess the ability to analyse complex information as the basis for good decision making. This talent is necessary to create a map or chessboard that defines the skills and abilities that must be present if a team is to achieve its goals. After creating the chessboard, the leader's next task is to identify the current skill profile of team members, noting where there is an abundance or a deficit of required abilities.

Asking team members to rate their own level of ability against the skills set out on the chessboard can be an interesting exercise. In the past, I have asked non-executive and executive board members to rate their proficiency against the skills needed within the board. This has been useful when a vacancy emerges or when the strategy becomes focused on a new challenge or opportunity.

These self-assessments might produce surprising results. Sometimes, team members reveal hidden skills and experience that were not previously evident to colleagues. The exercise also gives a leader a sense of how self-aware colleagues are. I recall noting that humble team members tended to underscore themselves and those lacking insight tended to overestimate their levels of expertise.

Many leaders find it interesting to incorporate the results of personality tests such as the Myers Briggs Type Indicator (MBTI), the Belbin Team Roles Test or the Hogan Personality Inventory into their analysis. This information can contribute a more rounded overview of individuals and enables a picture of team diversity or homogeneity to emerge.

The analysis process will also give an indication of balance or imbalance. A balanced team is diverse in its personality types, perspectives and experiences. It contains expertise covering all the skill squares.

Overall, this process helps identify the priority skills that need to be developed or attracted to the team if it is to be successful in achieving its goals.

Appealing to talent

It is worth remembering that the most talented applicants are drawn to an ambitious purpose and a culture that offers them the right fit. This reinforces the importance of a leader articulating clearly the purpose and goals of the organisation and the expected contribution of individuals, as described in Chapter 2.

It is vital that there is good alignment between what is put in recruitment materials and what prospective candidates actually experience. It takes time and careful thought to draft recruitment materials that are appealing, accurate and honest. This should not be rushed and should include relevant input from as wide a group as possible.

For example, when I was leading the recruitment of a chief executive, I gave every staff member an opportunity to identify the most important skills and qualities they hoped to see in the appointed person. The qualities they identified were analysed and incorporated into the candidate pack.

Most candidates value an opportunity to hold informal discussions prior to interview so that they can ask any questions they wish, get a feel for their potential colleagues and test whether they can see themselves working in the team. This is a good approach to support due diligence on both sides.

Preliminary conversations need to be informal and not determinative of a recruitment outcome. These conversations are not interviews by another name. Candidates need to know that if they apply, they are going to be treated fairly and will be on a level playing field.

When leading a chief executive recruitment process, I made sure every candidate had the same opportunity to hold informal conversations with as many directors, staff members and stakeholders as they wished. All the applicants made use of this offer. It was encouraging to receive feedback that informal conversations created a consistent impression that reflected the material in the candidate pack describing the organisation and the role.

Fair, wise recruitment practices

In the last decade, I have chaired forty appointment panels for the Judicial Appointments Commission (JAC). Our role as panel members is to assess candidates at a sift stage and at a selection stage so that the commissioners can make informed appointment decisions. It is fascinating and a pleasure to work with such interesting, capable people.

The JAC's purpose is to select judges based on merit and good character who reflect the diverse society they serve. It was created in part to address the negative consequences of using a 'tap on the shoulder' appointment process in the past.

The senior judicial roles filled by the JAC are lifetime appointments. If an error is made and a poor candidate is appointed, there are serious consequences. Lifetime-appointed judges cannot be removed. It is therefore unsurprising that the JAC is scrupulous in adhering to fair and merit-based selection processes.

During my induction, I was reminded more than once, 'If in doubt, do not appoint.' This was great advice which I have applied to all the appointment panels I have subsequently led or supported.

There are five elements to implementing fair recruitment processes:

1. Role definition

2. Mitigating bias

3. Sifting and shortlisting criteria

4. Appropriate selection methods

5. Fair decision making

1. Role definition

Without a clearly defined role specification, matching candidates to requirements fairly is nigh on impossible. The specification needs to set out in writing the must-haves in terms of qualifications, knowledge, skills and personal qualities. The decision makers must then use this specification to guide all stages of the recruitment process.

On JAC appointments, role specifications cover areas such as legal knowledge, judicial skills, personal qualities, communication skills and ability to manage work efficiently.

2. Mitigating bias

Working with the JAC has given me access to training in understanding bias and how it can be mitigated. The useful learning includes:

- Everyone is hard-wired to hold biases. This is an evolutionary feature of human brains enabling threats to be anticipated and affinity with the familiar to be automatic.

- Unconscious bias emerges more frequently when you are fatigued or working under time pressure.

- Awareness of personal biases mitigates the risk of casting a candidate in a more or less favourable light. For example, I learned that I have a bias in favour of extrovert, high-energy communicators. Awareness of this bias helps me check that I score and assess all candidates equitably, whether they are chatty or dour.

- Avoid comparing candidates. Assessing each individual consistently against a defined specification mitigates the risk of bias.

- Reminding yourself frequently to be fair and objective to all candidates can significantly mitigate the risk of unconscious bias affecting decision making.[13]

It is useful to identify potential bias risk areas at the outset and to discuss these risks and how they can be avoided with all involved in the recruitment process. For example, when it comes to judicial appointments, bias from assumptions may be linked to candidate gender or ethnicity, as well as background such as university, employing firm (solicitors), chambers (barristers), jurisdiction of legal expertise and previous judicial experience.

Discussing these potential risk areas at the outset makes it easier to resolve any issues that arise. This also helps panel members challenge any scores or comments that may be rooted in bias when they arise.

3. Sifting and shortlisting criteria

This area is closely linked to the role specification, which should define clearly the requirements for appointment. If there is a sifting or shortlisting step involved in the recruitment, there must be a fair, consistent way to assess written applications against the must-have requirements.

Sometimes the results of a qualifying test are used to shortlist. For most appointments, shortlisting is done on the basis of assessing a written application that includes a curriculum vitae (CV) and a statement of suitability. References may also be available at this stage.

When making appointments to non-judicial roles, I have read all applications and allocated them to one of three groups. An A candidate will have demonstrated in the written application that they possess the required qualities and should be interviewed. B candidates meet some of the requirements and should be discussed with panel members or decision makers. A C candidate does not meet the requirements and should not be shortlisted. Others may not meet eligibility criteria – such as possessing a specific qualification – and will be ruled out.

I always share all the applications and my grouping suggestions with panel members, and then come to an agreed outcome on the shortlist which is evidence-based and consistent.

4. Appropriate selection methods

There are many options to choose from when you are designing the best selection methods. Returning to the role specification and considering how a candidate can best demonstrate competence against that requirement is a good place to start.

Relying exclusively on a panel interview can be a risk. Using other methods to test competence presents a more rounded picture of candidates' abilities. For example, when I am appointing to a board role, I often like to set a **group task** that involves candidates reading a scenario and working with others to complete a task such as prioritising actions to develop a strategic plan or identifying risks in making an investment.

To be honest, the detail of the scenario involved is largely irrelevant. The important thing is that the task gives a fair test of the specific skills and abilities required of the role.

The group task commences after a set amount of time for reading the material and absorbing instructions. The group is then left alone to complete the task with observers noting individual contributions against the requirements of the role.

I like this exercise because it is analogous to the actual work of the board and reveals what candidates are really like when they are working in a group. So many times, this group work has allowed a candidate to shine by showing what they can do. Just as often, the exercise makes it easier to eliminate candidates who demonstrate a lack of key skills, poor behaviours or an inability to work as part of a team.

CASE STUDY – The value of group exercises

During one recruitment process for a non-executive director, there were enough candidates to hold two different group exercises. In the first group, a candidate who had been a member of parliament (MP) appointed himself to the role of chairing the group without discussion. He did a lot of pontificating and little listening, tried to dominate the task and showed exactly what he would be like to work with in a board environment.

One of the other candidates did a sterling job of politely challenging his approach and managed to keep the group on task. Guess which of these two individuals was ultimately appointed?

In the second group, although the exact same task and briefing were available, the exercise played out differently. In this group, the members asked one candidate to chair, and that individual demonstrated exceptional skill in collaborative working, bringing all the participants in and showing precisely how well-suited he was to working collegiately with others.

Within that group, there was one individual who had exceptional qualifications and was working in a university environment. Despite his intellectual ability, he demonstrated that he had not read the briefing properly. His contributions showed that he had failed to absorb the material correctly. Here, using a group exercise revealed a problem area. Relying solely on the written application would have made it easy to make incorrect assumptions and overestimate that individual's abilities.

The JAC uses **role plays** for what it deems entry-level judicial roles. These role plays involve candidates having a set amount of time to read a scenario with relevant legal and procedural information. They then enter a courtroom or tribunal with actors playing the roles of the parties in a hearing. They are required to conduct the hearing and to give a judgement within a set amount of time.

These role plays are designed to be a fair test of a candidate's ability to do the job for which they are applying. No question, most candidates find the role plays a daunting experience, but having observed hundreds of them, I am convinced that they are an excellent indicator of ability. The candidates who sail through impressively are careful in their preparation, organised in their approach, mindful of how they treat the parties and focused on gathering relevant information so they can reach a fair, reasoned decision.

I have seen many disasters as well. When candidates have not thought themselves adequately into the role of the judge, this tends to prove their undoing.

Overall, using a group exercise or a role play that puts a candidate into a simulation of the vacancy they aspire to fill is a useful element of the selection process, but this has to be a fair test, consistently applied. The design of the exercise is, therefore, crucial.

Specific things to consider include making sure that there is adequate preparation time for the candidates and clear instruction on the required task. Crucially, observers must be transparent and consistent in their approach. They must evaluate candidates against the specific role requirements and need to provide evidence for their conclusions.

Other methods can be incorporated depending on the qualities you seek to assess. If specific knowledge is a key requirement, a **qualifying test** may be appropriate. For communication skill, setting a task to give a **presentation** and answer questions may be a good choice. If stakeholder engagement is to be tested, holding a **focus group** or a 'speed dating' session with candidates discussing a single topic may be fitting. Again, making sure every method is properly designed, consistently applied and fairly assessed is crucial.

Most selection processes incorporate a **panel interview**. The aim should be to create an environment where every candidate can perform at their best. This means setting aside adequate time for panel members to agree their approach and questions beforehand.

There is nothing wrong or soft in making candidates feel welcome and at ease. They are much more likely to relax and perform well if the panel is *not* adversarial, trying to catch them out or asking trick questions. Such ruses are unpleasant and will make the candidate legitimately question whether they really want to work with you.

Past experience is the clearest predictor of future performance, so taking a competence-based approach to set interview questions is the best route. This means asking candidates to give specific examples that illustrate they possess the qualities featuring on the must haves in the role specification.

For example, you can ask candidates to tell you about a time when they did, dealt with or achieved something relevant to the required abilities. Follow-up questions can probe the candidate's thought process, what the outcome was, how they worked with others, what they learned or what they would do differently if faced with the same situation. Framing questions in this way guards against waffle and hypothetical answers. This approach provides more reliable evidence of the candidate's abilities.

You will get much better results if candidates know that this is the approach you plan to take for the panel interview. Sharing this approach with candidates in advance means they have time to think about their experience and identify relevant examples that they can discuss during the interview. Having said that, even with judicial candidates who know the interview will be competence-based, many struggle with the format.

There are several difficulties you may encounter with competence-based interviewing.

The uncomfortable tumbleweed moment when a question is asked and the candidate **goes blank**. To deal with this, you can just pause in silence and wait for the candidate to call an example to mind. If that doesn't look like it is going to happen, you might see if you can develop a prompt from the written application.

For example, you might say, 'In your application, you told us about xyz. Would you like to develop that further and share the skill you demonstrated in that activity?' Sometimes, the dazed and blank look stays fixed. All you can do in that situation is say, 'Let's move on to another question. If we have time, we can return to this topic later.'

A second problem is the **'we'** answer. Candidates who are humble and genuine team players will often answer with reference to 'we did this' and 'we did that'. You want to know about the individual in front of you. Use prompts to nudge them to talk about themselves in the first person, perhaps by saying, 'You've mentioned "we" a lot in your answer so far. Tell me more about what you did personally and what your thought process was in that situation.'

The 'I didn't listen to the question properly' answer. Surprisingly, this happens a lot. Candidates listen to the first words of a question and seize on them rather than taking in fully what has been asked of them.

I noticed this happened in recent interviews when the question was quite long. A colleague asked for an example of integrity, and then for details of an unpopular or difficult decision with some specific characteristics. A number of candidates asked for the question to be repeated. Invariably, they gave better answers. For others, they homed in on one part only, describing an unpopular decision they had made.

These answers did not always address the question that was asked.

The lesson learned is that shorter, more concise questions work better. Ask a brief question relating to the skill you want to test, and then leave time to probe further into the answer. You can also say politely, 'What I am trying to understand is your experience of (skill). Can you tell us about a time you demonstrated that ability?'

The long ramble answer. This happens most often when a candidate does not really have experience of the specific skill being tested and they feel compelled to waffle on about anything and everything vaguely connected to the topic. You might also get the long ramble when a candidate has really warmed to the topic and wants to tell you everything they know, even if it is not really relevant.

For example, in answer to a question on diversity and demonstrating respect for difference, a candidate gave us a long-winded, wide-ranging answer. He wandered from challenging an unpleasant remark about a gay colleague to a homily on understanding others' 'operating systems', to the Black Lives Matter movement, to police conduct in the USA, to reading books, to being an ally, to reporting individuals to their professional bodies for holding intolerant views about the use of Pride logos on email footers. It was a whirlwind tour. My colleague kindly summarised this as an awareness of diversity and a willingness to tackle discrimination.

The 'Here's one I prepared earlier' (literally) answer. Many times, candidates will bring notes to the interview with them – maybe a copy of their statement or a bullet list to remind them of the examples they might draw on in framing their answer. Personally, I have no problem with a candidate bringing a crib sheet if they find this helpful. As the interviewer, you are hoping they will choose good examples that provide sound evidence of their abilities. Who cares if they draw on a note to remind them of the points they want to make?

However, I was really surprised in a recent interview to see that in a large pile of notes, the candidate had typed out full-page answers to numerous possible questions. On two occasions, he actually read out the typed answer verbatim to the panel. He did not look up from his note and did not pause for breath. It was like watching someone read an academic essay aloud. Needless to say, this was a very poor choice of communication method. I have not seen that one before, and I hope not to experience it again!

Whether the answers have been great or terrible, you want to draw the interview to an end professionally. The interview is the last time decision makers will see the candidates, so thanking them for their interest and application and setting expectations about what happens next is the best way to end on a positive note.

5. Fair decision making

Great leaders see every recruitment exercise as an opportunity to showcase their organisation among potential
fans. They expect every candidate to enjoy the recruitment process and to leave with a positive impression of
the organisation, even if they do not succeed in being
appointed. They genuinely hope to have a tough choice
to make, having attracted a strong field of applicants.

These outcomes do not happen by accident, so it is
imperative to design processes carefully and, above all,
to make fair, evidence-based decisions. Decision makers
should review input from each method they have used
as part of the recruitment. They should have an opportunity to discuss and evaluate the information and be
able to articulate a clear rationale for their decision.

There are different theories about the best time to bring
in references. Having access to references at an early
stage can help decision makers identify areas to probe
during the recruitment process. For other roles – particularly those when people apply on the basis that their
candidacy is not known by their current employer – it
may be more appropriate to take up references for a
preferred candidate after they have been appointed;
make the appointment subject to references in these
instances, just in case there is a problem.

Great leaders know that the process must have integrity and that reaching the right decision is vital.

Appointing the wrong person can be hugely damaging and expensive in terms of time, money and goodwill.

CASE STUDY – How not to make a decision

As a management team member, I was once asked to serve on an appointment panel with my newly promoted chief executive and a human resources (HR) colleague. We were recruiting a project manager to lead the implementation of an important business service.

There were two candidates. The first, an external candidate, had a good track record of similar work in another sector. He had strong opinions on how the service should be developed. The second was an internal candidate who had been a long-standing colleague of the chief executive.

At the end of the interview, the chief executive pushed the paperwork aside, saying there was no need for a discussion as it was obvious the internal candidate would be appointed. She said, 'We are going to select Bob. He's a creep, but I like creeps. They tell you what you want to hear.'

This experience proved to be a turning point, giving me an insight into the values of my new boss. I did not stay long in that organisation. I was very sad to leave a great business with fantastic colleagues, but I did not feel I could work in that culture.

Depending on the role, there may be external interference that can impact fair decision making.

74

CASE STUDY – Never compromise on your integrity

In my last role, an MP tried to undermine the recruitment of a new chief executive at a late stage. A couple of days before the final interviews, she sent me an urgent text demanding to know who the candidates were. She alleged that staff and stakeholders had not been involved and that the recruitment process was corrupt.

This was patently untrue. I explained in detail what the process had been, but I refused to name individual candidates. This provoked an onslaught of angry responses, accusing me of running a secret service akin to the KGB and making various threats if I failed to name the candidates.

Although I knew there was a significant risk of incurring a wrathful response, I refused to take the easy road of naming the candidates. I knew the recruitment process was properly constructed, fair and robust. It was compliant with good practice and proper governance standards.

Above all, the candidates involved were all employed in other organisations and had an entirely reasonable expectation that their identities would be kept confidential. They had been told that the process would not be played out in the media, that their names would not be treated as gossip fodder and that they could determine when they wished to discuss their applications with their current employers and colleagues.

The surest way to trigger withdrawn applications is to leak identities, offer a running commentary on candidates and/or permit inappropriate external interference. This behaviour tells candidates that your recruitment process lacks integrity and that you cannot be trusted to produce a fair and evidence-based decision.

In the end, the process resulted in the appointment of an outstanding candidate, much to the delight of staff, stakeholders and the board. The MP never spoke to me again which was an added bonus.

Warm welcomes

Having gone through the process of choosing a recruit, the strong leader's next task is to make sure there are onboarding arrangements to help the new colleague get off to a good start.

In my last organisation with about 14,000 employees, an analysis of exit interviews and feedback from recent recruits showed some startling gaps. The organisation was pretty much in a constant process of recruitment, but was losing people at about the same rate it was making new appointments. A key member of staff delved into why this was the case and identified a real deficiency in onboarding arrangements.

She found that an enormous amount of effort was put into attracting applicants, but then, once appointment letters were sent out, it all went quiet. Many new recruits were unclear about absolute basics such as their start date, who their manager was, where their working base would be, where they should park, what they should wear and what their working hours would be.

From those who left the organisation within thirty days of joining, the feedback was equally poor. They described a real disconnect between what they were expecting and what they actually experienced. Many could not log-in to IT systems; they could not get an ID badge that opened doors to their area of work; they were not paid correctly or on time; they did not receive appropriate inductions; they did not feel welcome or part of the team.

Some of the key things that made a difference included:

- Providing a welcome pack to all new recruits that answered questions, explained the staff wellbeing offer and gave contact details of how to get help for any concerns.

- Providing a 'Welcome to the Team' postcard with a personal message that was signed by the line manager and new colleagues.

- Providing training to all line managers to set out their role in welcoming and supporting new team members; providing a week one and week four check in; and setting clear objectives aligned to purpose and goals.

- Arranging an online induction for all new recruits to give a welcome from leaders, to provide an overview of the organisation, to cover essential information, to answer questions and to provide a chance to meet new colleagues in similar roles.

- Resolving logistical problems such as access to IT systems.

The poor practice that was creating such dissatisfaction and high turnover among recruits was methodically addressed, resulting in much better feedback from new staff and a much lower attrition rate.

Sustaining the team

Once you have built your winning team, it is important to shift your mindset from recruitment to retention. Successful teams need ongoing support from their leader to thrive.

There are five key areas that require your attention:

1. Remuneration

2. Review and future focus

3. Team building and development

4. Talent management

5. Succession planning

1. Remuneration

You will need to set initial pay competitively, and then apply fair, transparent pay review processes to continue to recognise and reward your team appropriately.

CASE STUDY – The importance of fairness in the pay review

In my first management consultant role, I worked for a firm that reviewed pay annually. We would each receive a letter from the managing director indicating our new pay banding.

After I had been working for the company for a couple of years, I was disappointed to receive a pay review that was just £1 short of putting me into the next pay banding. This would not have cost the company much, but it would have given me one key benefit. Moving into the next banding meant I could choose my company car.

As the only female consultant on the team, I was treated differently. Not only was my pay set below that of my colleagues, who had less experience, I was the only consultant who had to drive a hand-me-down company car, rather than choosing a new car on appointment.

I raised this with my boss and requested an additional £1 pay increase and the option of choosing a car. My request was denied with a fairly spineless excuse about not setting precedents.

Two months later, one of my clients offered me a fantastic job with much enhanced pay and benefits. When I handed in my resignation, suddenly I was such a valued employee that the firm could not bear to lose me. Instantly, my boss was able to match my new offer, including ordering any car I liked.

I genuinely wanted to take on the new opportunity and was not using the job offer as a negotiating position, so I declined to stay, but the irony of the situation did not escape me. Ever since, I have been mindful of the importance of fairness in reviewing pay and making sure the approach taken does not send mixed messages.

It is always much more costly to replace a valued employee than it is to meet their reasonable expectations.

2. Review and future focus

You must undertake regular reviews with each direct report on a six-monthly or more frequent basis. These reviews give you the chance to share meaningful observations on past performance and to agree future objectives. This is the best opportunity you will have to provide lasting motivation to individuals by recognising what they have done well and how you can support them to address any gaps. You also have the opportunity to customise their personal objectives. Future objectives should draw on their strengths and connect their work directly to the organisation's purpose and goals.

3. Team building and development

Regular reviews should include time to identify areas for personal and team development. People find investment in their personal development highly motivating. Supporting your team members to learn, grow and improve individually and collectively will pay dividends in terms of retention, productivity and morale.

Investing in development is the best way to build a cohesive team where all members feel valued, included and a sense of belonging. Team development also builds mature understanding among colleagues, enabling the creative analysis and debate that result in good decision making.

4. Talent management

Having a talent management programme can be a great way to identify individuals with potential who can take on new or hard-to-fill roles. This can help build a pipeline of diverse talent for future needs. Equally, if you are at risk of losing talented colleagues to competitors, introducing a talent management approach can assist with retention.

A successful talent management programme requires a clear rationale and careful implementation to avoid sowing discord among individuals who may feel unhappy that they are not included in the programme.

5. Succession planning

It is never too soon to start planning for the future. Colleagues will have a legitimate interest in how their careers can develop. A wise leader nurtures ambition by giving others development opportunities and structured advice on career progression.

This is also a time to bring your leadership skills in horizon scanning and analysis to bear in looking at how job roles will evolve and change over time. For example, the rapid development of artificial intelligence (AI) technologies will mean significant change for everyone in the workplace. Part of your leadership role is to respond to these changes proactively with sound planning.

When it all goes horribly wrong

Despite your best efforts to build and sustain a winning team, it is inevitable that something will go wrong at some stage. Leadership involves working with humans, so it will not always be sweetness and light.

I guarantee that every leadership journey characterised by success, wins and harmony will also, at some stage, be punctuated by the odd mistake, conflict or disaster. You cannot prevent these problems from ever occurring, but through your leadership, you can mitigate their impact, frame a positive response and accelerate recovery. Taking quick and appropriate action is the best antidote to the negative consequences these problems can bring.

There are five typical problems that can undermine your winning team:

1. **External change.** This might include losing a contract, a shift in market conditions or a regulatory or political change that impacts the organisation and work of the team.

2. **Square pegs in round holes.** This is when an individual's skills, values or behaviours are not aligned to needs. This problem may emerge when new requirements are met with a defensive or inflexible response.

3. **Performance gaps.** This is when an individual is struggling to perform to the standards or expectations that have been agreed. Sometimes underperformance is caused by personal problems spilling into work life. Sometimes underperformance is rooted in a genuine need for training or for more help to achieve tasks, and sometimes, underperformance is caused by refusal to work hard. It requires sensitivity and good judgement to establish the specific cause of performance gaps in each case.

4. **Personality clashes.** This is when individuals within the team fail to understand each other. The resulting friction damages individual and collective performance and morale.

5. **Misconduct.** This is wilful failure to observe required standards of behaviour and conduct.

Typically, misconduct involves a breach of ethical standards or an abuse of power.

When these problems arise, the Firecracker Leader responds by marshalling all of their head, hands and heart abilities. For example, you will need curiosity and your analytical skills to understand what is at the root of the problem. Once you have gathered facts and have asked why questions, then you can begin to frame and communicate solutions with compassion and understanding. Keep an open mind and try not to make assumptions about what is at the root of the problem. Ask open questions and listen carefully.

It is always a good idea to take professional advice on the course of action you deem is best. The most important thing is to take action. A great leader will not let problems fester. Although it can be deeply uncomfortable to raise and address problems, not dealing with them always creates much worse consequences.

CASE STUDY – Supportive leadership

I was aware of problems in one organisation where an important capital development project was facing disaster. The board was increasingly concerned at the lack of credible plans to complete the project, which seemed beset by risk. Every time the team responsible for the project came to give an update on their work, the board's confidence was further depleted.

The individual tasked with leading the team was quite simply overwhelmed and pulled in too many directions to be effective. This lack of clarity and focus undermined the whole team's ability to function properly.

The board brought in a new team leader with a single objective: to get the project back on track. The new leader approached the task by gathering information from all the team members about the reasons for the poor performance and asking how they felt about their roles.

The team leader acting on this diagnostic resulted in a completely different environment within the team. With mature leadership, the team members felt supported and trusted. They were comfortable discussing problems and risks openly so that solutions could be identified.

In the end, the same people who had been overwhelmed and confused appeared to have been replaced by improved, more confident versions of themselves. The injection of supportive leadership and clarity enabled the team to complete the project.

Gross misconduct and wilful underperformance are, fortunately, rare occurrences. Most people come to work every day wanting to do a good job. Having an open conversation is the first step to finding a constructive resolution when things are heading in the wrong direction.

However, on the odd occasion, you may be badly let down by others.

CASE STUDY – The suspicious absentee

I recall having this experience in an early operational leadership role. One of the managers in the business unit I was leading had been off sick for some time. My HR director mentioned that she was concerned about the lack of detail available around the cause of his absence. She suggested that she conduct a home visit to meet with the manager and find out more about how he could be supported to return to work.

A week later, she shared with me the detailed notes from her meeting. The manager had a severe gastro-intestinal complaint that meant he was housebound and could not be more than a few metres away from the bathroom. His diet was greatly restricted, and he could only consume bland foods in tiny quantities. Some ingredients – such as meat, dairy and alcohol – caused painful symptoms to flare up, and he had had to remove these items from his diet.

My colleague said something did not ring true during her visit. She had grown increasingly suspicious about how genuine his illness was. She suggested hiring a private detective to follow and film the manager if he left his home.

The results were astonishing. A week later, she played the video for me.

First up was a scene of this apparently desperately ill, bathroom-bound person gambolling out of his house, wearing white shorts and a t-shirt. He drove to a local printing shop and left a leaflet with the shop to be copied.

The next scene was of him sitting in a café, eating a fry up. While he was enjoying his plate laden with bacon, eggs, sausages, fried bread and beans, the detective returned to the printing shop and saw the leaflets he had ordered. He was marketing stag dos in Blackpool as a side hustle!

The manager returned home for a while. He was next filmed in the early afternoon, sitting in the garden of a pub drinking lager and eating crisps and peanuts with a group of friends.

At this stage, the detective suggested my HR colleague phone him to ask how he was. The recording included all of his answers, confirming he was still terribly unwell and unable to leave the house. After the phone call, he laughed with his mates and said he intended to keep the scam going until his six months of full pay and six months of half pay had run out.

I still recall the feeling of incredulity I had while watching the video. Some of the scenes were hugely comical given they were the exact opposite of his described state of illness. Watching him wolf down a massive fried breakfast was beyond belief.

Needless to say, the manager was sent a letter of dismissal on the grounds of gross misconduct. Surprisingly, he appealed against his dismissal. My HR colleague was looking forward to playing the video for him during the appeal hearing. She never got to do this as he withdrew the appeal a few days before it was due to be held.

This is the only case of its kind that I have encountered in over thirty years of senior leadership roles, so

I want to stress that it is the exception, not the rule. It is good to have faith in human nature and to expect people to behave honestly and with integrity, especially about something like a serious illness. However, when trust is betrayed, it is equally important to take decisive action.

I felt it was necessary to share the detail of this case with all the staff in my business unit. I wanted them to know that the company's generous sick pay scheme was there to support all of us if and when we were genuinely unwell, but any abuse of it would naturally make it harder to sustain the terms that were set for all our benefit.

Through his actions, our former colleague had betrayed all our trust.

Summary

This chapter has described the six steps to building a winning team:

- Identifying in overview all the skills the team needs.

- Attracting the best, most diverse talent.

- Using fair recruitment practices.

- Providing support and a warm welcome to new colleagues.

- Investing wisely and fairly in ongoing development.

- Acting decisively and sensitively when there are problems.

The Firecracker Leader	The Poor Leader
• Takes a strategic approach to defining skill requirements and understanding team morale • Is comfortable appointing talented experts who shine • Is committed to fair recruitment practices that are robust and have integrity • Welcomes and supports team members • Tackles underperformance, conflict and poor behaviours fairly and decisively	• Fails to analyse and forecast skill needs • Feels threatened by others' excellence • Makes appointments that do not upset status quo or personal comfort zones (masquerading as fit) • Goes through the motions on recruitment processes • Gossips about candidates • Lacks curiosity in understanding reasons for turnover, low commitment, underperformance or poor morale • Succumbs to external pressure

This chapter has covered the following Firecracker Leadership Framework attributes:

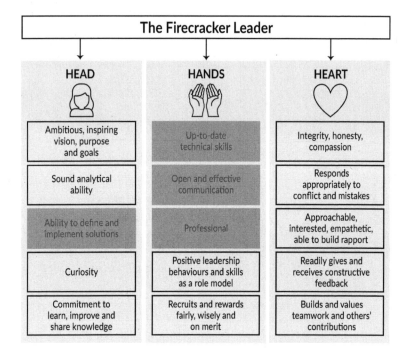

The Firecracker Leader		
HEAD	**HANDS**	**HEART**
Ambitious, inspiring vision, purpose and goals	Up-to-date technical skills	Integrity, honesty, compassion
Sound analytical ability	Open and effective communication	Responds appropriately to conflict and mistakes
Ability to define and implement solutions	Professional	Approachable, interested, empathetic, able to build rapport
Curiosity	Positive leadership behaviours and skills as a role model	Readily gives and receives constructive feedback
Commitment to learn, improve and share knowledge	Recruits and rewards fairly, wisely and on merit	Builds and values teamwork and others' contributions

FOUR

How To Celebrate Good Times

G reat leaders know how important recognition and celebration are to building an engaged, high-performing workforce and a positive organisational culture. They know that sincere, genuine praise is a powerful motivator.

Quite simply, people leave organisations when they do not feel valued and appreciated. The corollary is also true: employees will stay in even the most challenged organisations when they feel part of something worthwhile and their efforts are recognised sincerely and appropriately.

Leaders are no different to everyone else in that they want to be valued and appreciated for what they do.

This is why it is so surprising when leaders make the mistake of only paying lip service to wins and achievements and dwell exclusively on problems. They err in thinking celebration is a nice-to-have or inappropriate.

Nothing could be further from the truth. All positive behaviours are reinforced through recognition, so the best way to encourage more achievement is to recognise even small wins by celebrating who and what created them.

Insecure leaders fear they will look soft if they show appreciation and praise people. They worry that they will be labelled 'Pollyanna' or 'Pangloss', characters cursed with such an excess of naïve optimism that even catastrophes were celebrated as being wonderful and all for the best.

Great leaders do not pretend everything is always rosy. They tell the truth and are comfortable showcasing genuine achievement and encouraging effort to make improvements where needed.

The confident leader knows that recognising others' achievement is one of the most powerful tools they possess. The author Dale Carnegie wrote, 'Nothing else so inspires or heartens people as words of appreciation.'[14] Dale Carnegie was also careful to remind readers that praise must be honest, sincere and evidence-based. People can spot a phony or an ulterior motive a mile off.

Appreciation must be authentic, genuine and specific if it is to land well and meaningfully. Flattery creates the opposite impact of sincere praise, making people feel suspicious and uncomfortable.

Of course, the methods of recognition and celebration need to be proportionate and sensitive to the prevailing environment. If resources are tight, there are plenty of low-cost, high-impact ways to celebrate and express sincere appreciation that make people feel good. This chapter describes some of those approaches so celebration and recognition become part of business as usual. These approaches are crucial to build confidence and good morale. Some additional ideas for building long-lasting positive impact are also provided.

The chapter describes four methods of celebrating, recognising and appreciating the efforts of others:

1. Using symbols

2. Showcasing key events

3. Building celebration and gratitude into daily life

4. When highlighting the bad is good

Using symbols

Even small gestures can convey great meaning.

CASE STUDY – The double decker award

In my first managing director role, I was responsible for winning a franchise to establish a new business integrating staff from six separate organisations. To build cohesion and ownership of the business's overall purpose and strategy, I presented a monthly team brief. I would report honestly on all aspects of performance, identifying successes as well as the areas needing more effort and attention.

The balance was on highlighting positive achievements to invite recognition for the colleagues involved. This reflected the saying that 'a rising tide raises all ships', meaning everyone benefits by recognising and celebrating instances of success, even where these occur outside their own teams.

One month, I described the achievement of one particular performance goal and called up the individual who had contributed significantly. I presented him with a Double Decker, an inexpensive chocolate bar, that for some reason I had an instinct to buy from a vending machine on my way to the meeting. The applause and celebration for that individual were genuine and spontaneous, and I was pleasantly surprised by the number of staff who asked if the following month there would be another Double Decker presentation.

The awarding of the Double Decker became part of our monthly routine. There was nothing particularly special about the chocolate bar itself, but it was an important symbol, vesting meaning for colleagues who saw it as an appropriate way to appreciate and celebrate achievement.

CASE STUDY – Who would like a sticker?

Many years later, in one of my NHS chair roles, I had an instinct to use the power of the symbol again. Following a positive Care Quality Commission (CQC) inspection that had been particularly gruelling for the organisation, a sandwich lunch was arranged for the staff who were involved in hosting the inspectors and making the process work seamlessly.

On my way into the trust, I stopped at a local supermarket and bought a £1 bag of foam stickers with hearts and stars on them. I said a few words of sincere thanks to the attendees on behalf of the board and joked that no expense had been spared in bestowing a sticker on those who would like one to wear on their ID badge – just a little visible symbol of gratitude and appreciation in recognition of their efforts. To my surprise, every attendee queued up and requested a sticker.

The next day the word had got out, and I was inundated with requests for a sticker from those who were unable to attend the lunch.

The small chocolate bar and the little foam sticker in these two case studies became meaningful symbols because they represented sincere gratitude and recognition.

Showcasing key events

Significant events often provide a fitting backdrop to the most effective celebrations. Leaders who are in close touch with their people may develop an intuitive sense for the most appropriate way to celebrate.

CASE STUDY – Serving those who serve

I had the pleasure of working with a particularly effective chief executive who really understood how to make people feel valued and special. She had an instinctive knack of knowing how best to arrange the spotlight on others.

On one occasion, she asked if I would fill in for her at a luncheon to thank volunteers and recognise their service. A diary conflict meant she could not take part in the event, and I willingly agreed to sub for her. As expected, I was asked to say a few words and to present plaques to those who had given long service, but I was taken aback when I was told the main requirement was to wear comfortable shoes.

It turned out that this chief executive had started a tradition of directors personally serving the meal to the many volunteers who attended this annual event. I was glad to be reminded to wear the right shoes because it certainly was a workout! What a great way to celebrate. It was an event that showcased the honour of serving those who serve.

I cannot think of a more significant and challenging experience than coping with the COVID-19 pandemic. For those working in healthcare, particularly in urban areas, this was the most testing time imaginable. At my own NHS trust in Liverpool, the staff were utterly heroic in their response to this most frightening of events.

One of my colleagues had all the right instincts in suggesting how the board could recognise and celebrate the courage, compassion and teamwork that were the hallmark of the organisation's response. He recommended we provided four things to all 14,000 members of staff: a thank you cupcake, a thank you card, a thank you pin, and a hoody embroidered with the trust's name and the NHS rainbow.

Although there were some challenges – sourcing and delivering 14,000 inscribed iced cupcakes is no mean feat – it was a fitting gesture which was much appreciated. The feedback from staff was very positive, and it is lovely to see how many people still wear their hoodies with pride. Some staff even arranged for their names to be embroidered on their hoodies under the trust's name, reflecting their sense of connection to an organisation that handled such a significant event so well.

CASE STUDY – We are the champions!

Mid-pandemic, Liverpool Football Club offered to bring the newly won Premiership trophy to the trust sites, allowing staff to be photographed with it and a background reading, 'We are Liverpool, you are our champions'. It was a fabulous occasion with countless members of staff standing in socially distanced queues waiting to have their photograph taken. Not everyone can count on their local club winning the Premiership, but when such an opportunity presents itself, it is wise to piggyback on it.

More recently, one of the Merseyside local authorities awarded the Freedom of the Borough to the healthcare organisations that cared for residents during the pandemic. A representative group of staff from each healthcare organisation was invited to attend the presentation, which was a lovely, heartfelt occasion. The staff who attended felt proud and suggested that the scroll presented to the organisation was taken on a tour of all the hospital sites. They wanted all colleagues to be included and to share the recognition in being awarded the local authority's highest honour.

CASE STUDY – Showcasing small achievements

It does not have to be a global pandemic or a massive success that prompts celebration. At a seminar on performance improvement, one chief executive described how he led his organisation to overcome serious problems to such an extent that it successfully exited stringent regulatory restrictions.

He emphasised the critical importance of celebrating everything – even the smallest achievement – to build a sense of momentum and belief within the organisation. Nothing is too small to be showcased. In his own words, he said he would 'turn up to the opening of an envelope' with a photographer and a press release at the ready. Every small win was an opportunity to congratulate others and to reinforce understanding that the organisation had turned a corner and had the ability to overcome its problems.

This leader had really embraced the process of building confidence and capability incrementally. He understood that showcasing small achievements would generate a shared belief that larger goals were achievable.

Building celebration and gratitude into daily life

There is a reason why staff noticeboards often display thank you cards. The simple act of saying thank you in writing is always received with great appreciation.

My son is a GP in the North East of England. He shared this card he received from a five-year-old patient with a message saying, This made my day!:

When the sentiment is so genuine, that is all that matters. Regional words and phonetic spellings are certainly irrelevant.

Smart organisations recognise how motivating it is to receive genuine thanks and have created electronic systems to make it easy for thank you messages to be created and shared. In one business, a thoughtful in-house team designed an electronic thank you post-card that could be sent to any member of staff on the internal address list. This was popular among senders and recipients.

Also in this business, a senior member of staff created a tradition of leaving on people's desks a mug filled with sweets and little gifts with a tag that read: 'You've been mugged!' The message expressed a thank you for the recipient's specific contribution and encouraged them to refill and anonymously 'mug' someone else who deserved a thank you.

In another organisation, a weekly Thank You Thursday email was circulated to all staff. The message contained a digest of all the separate thank you messages written from staff to their colleagues, as well as a capture of positive social media posts.

Distributing Employee of the Month and Team of the Month awards was a real highlight of my last role. Individuals and teams were nominated by colleagues, patients, families and partner organisations for their great work. Many of the nominations conveyed just how big a difference the recipients made through their work, particularly for people at a vulnerable and uncertain time.

For these presentations, colleagues would gather round to hear me read out the nominations and to celebrate the great example the recipients set of caring professionalism. It was a privilege to present the awards and to be part of the celebration photos.

When highlighting the bad is good

Celebrating individuals who speak up about things that are not right is of huge benefit in creating a positive organisational culture.

A member of staff identified that a group of patients who failed to attend one appointment were not being automatically rebooked for a second time. Individuals who had been referred by their GP for suspected cancers were at risk of harm if their diagnosis and treatment were delayed.

Although this instance represented a failure, the board felt strongly that the individual who had identified the problem should be recognised and celebrated for having called it out. The board agreed this example should be shared throughout the organisation to signal that it was safe and welcome to speak up when things were not right.

This is not celebrating mistakes and failures. It is celebrating a culture where an individual feels safe to do the right thing, even when it brings bad news. Speaking up about poor practice and problems is an indicator of psychological safety and a commitment to address and learn from mistakes.

The fallout from the Lucy Letby murder trial is a cautionary tale on this theme.[15] This nurse was found guilty of killing seven babies, which prompted questions about how her colleagues who had raised concerns were treated. It is so important that leaders listen carefully and act appropriately when concerns and problems are raised.

Ephemera vs lasting impact

The sections above contain ideas for getting into the habit of celebrating wins and enabling a culture of appreciation to become the norm. These approaches provide hits of motivation and positivity, but they have their limits. The feel-good factor associated with these celebrations is valuable, but essentially ephemeral.

Long-lasting positive impact is achieved when the expression of appreciation is sincere, specific, personalised and deeply felt. A leadership development session led by an expert facilitator provided a good learning experience in how to create this long-lasting impact.

CASE STUDY – Appreciation that lasts

As a new management team, my colleagues and I were building our knowledge of good practice and completing a variety of exercises to apply this information to our business. Throughout the session, there was a great atmosphere of camaraderie and fun that enabled trust and collegiate relationships to flourish.

One of the exercises in particular helped with this process of getting to know and trust each other. We went on a long ramble through the countryside and were instructed to walk in pairs in ten-minute bursts before changing walking partners. During our paired walk, we were each asked to share one positive attribute of our colleague and one thing we wanted less of in their contribution.

Being outside, walking side by side with a colleague, rather than sitting in an office on opposite sides of a desk or table, created an entirely different dynamic for good communication. Parents who have had productive conversations with their children while driving will recognise what I mean. Sitting in the car side by side, without direct eye contact, seems to enable a different level of discussion and openness.

The approach was liberating and served as a catalyst for exchanging honest information, conveyed with sensitivity and insight. I have used this walking exercise many times since. It is effective in building trust, and it is particularly useful if there are tensions that need to be surfaced carefully and without damaging anyone's self-esteem.

At the end of the week, we were asked to take part in one final exercise. We each wrote our name at the top of a piece of paper in front of us on the conference room table. We then moved to each person's paper in turn and were invited to go to the bottom of the page and write down one reason why we were glad that that individual was in the team. Then we were told to fold over our answer, leaving the next line above blank for another entry.

After rotating to every person's sheet of paper in turn, we each had a full list of positive observations about what we brought to the team and why that was appreciated by colleagues. Years later, one of the members of the team confided to me that he kept that piece of paper in his desk drawer and, if he ever had a bad day or a moment of self-doubt, he would read through it and would feel a renewed sense of optimism and confidence.

I have always treated six-month reviews and annual appraisals as an opportunity to capture in discussion and then in writing those occasions when a colleague did something worthy of recognition. Providing examples of their good practice enhances the value of the exercise and creates a lasting record of their achievement.

To be effective, the observations have to be specific. This requires careful thought and preparation. It's no good telling someone, 'Oh, you're great. You always do a super job.' This is transitory and fluffy. If you recount the specific time that they did xyz and the specific impact this created and how it affected you and others, you are on to meaningful observations that can stick. Capturing these observations on paper and making it part of the written record of your meeting enhances the significance and heft of your praise.

Maya Angelou is often credited with saying that people won't remember your words or actions, but they will remember how you made them feel. However, sometimes people only tell you how you made them feel when you leave!

Over the years, I have had some fabulous leaving parties. I was once treated to a send-off billed as *Bye, Bye*

Miss American Pie with all my colleagues coming dressed as their favourite American. During the event, I was given a *This is Your Life* presentation by a colleague dressed as John McEnroe, complete with tennis whites, a curly wig and a headband. That was a great night indeed.

I have always found that it is the cards with personal messages that create powerful memories and emotions because they convey how others were made to feel. One team of wonderful young women created a parting gift for me that I appreciate so much. This framed definition reminds me of them and makes me feel amazing every time I look at it:

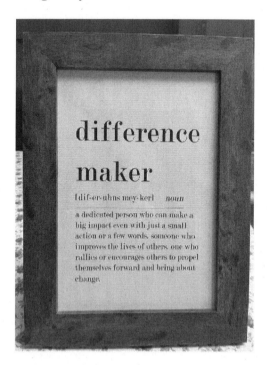

If you want to create a lasting sense of appreciation, be generous and share the specifics of how others' actions made you feel.

Summary

This chapter has described the importance of celebration and sincere appreciation in creating motivation and building a positive organisational culture. It shared four approaches to make celebration business as usual:

- Using symbols

- Showcasing key events

- Building celebration and gratitude into daily life

- When highlighting the bad is good

It also described the limitations of ephemeral celebrations and the long-lasting impact that specific, meaningful feedback creates.

The Firecracker Leader	The Poor Leader
• Generously gives credit to others and shines the spotlight on their achievements • Celebrates every win, including small things	• Glosses over wins in favour of focusing on problems • Fears looking soft and fluffy by recognising others' achievements

The Firecracker Leader	The Poor Leader
• Trusts their instincts to convey sincere, genuine appreciation	• Lacks generosity in praising others
• Makes celebration and recognition a feature of routine practice	• Steals the credit and fails to put the spotlight on others
• Considers and prepares feedback to others that is meaningful and has long-lasting impact	• Trades in cheap flattery or generalisations that lack sincerity and depth

This chapter has covered the following Firecracker Leadership Framework attributes:

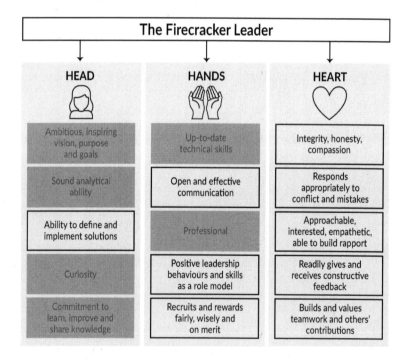

The Firecracker Leader		
HEAD	**HANDS**	**HEART**
Ambitious, inspiring vision, purpose and goals	Up-to-date technical skills	Integrity, honesty, compassion
Sound analytical ability	Open and effective communication	Responds appropriately to conflict and mistakes
Ability to define and implement solutions	Professional	Approachable, interested, empathetic, able to build rapport
Curiosity	Positive leadership behaviours and skills as a role model	Readily gives and receives constructive feedback
Commitment to learn, improve and share knowledge	Recruits and rewards fairly, wisely and on merit	Builds and values teamwork and others' contributions

FIVE
How To Cope With Crisis

'The most fortunate of us all in our journey through life frequently meet with calamities and misfortunes which may greatly afflict us: and to fortify our minds against the attacks of these calamities and misfortunes should be one of the principal studies and endeavors of our lives.'
   Thomas Jefferson[16]

'In every crisis, doubt or confusion, take the higher path – the path of compassion, courage, understanding and love.'
   Amit Ray[17]

These two quotes are instructive on how to cope with crisis. Their message reflects the head, hands, heart philosophy of Firecracker Leadership.

First, accept that crises are an inevitable part of life (head). Second, prepare for the inevitable by developing the skills you will need (hands). Third, approach every crisis with empathy and emotional intelligence (heart).

This chapter describes the kinds of disasters you may face as a leader at work, in your personal life and in the wider world. It provides examples that offer practical tips to help you manage the most testing of situations.

Work disasters

Coping with disaster is a fundamental leadership skill. All manner of things can and will go wrong during your leadership career, and it is important to cultivate the ability to manage these situations calmly. The more experience you have of coping when things go wrong, the more confident you become in your own ability and the more intuition you develop about managing in the moment.

Interestingly, the more proficient you become in managing a work crisis, the fewer crises actually arise. This is because your personal threshold for what constitutes a crisis is raised in proportion to your experience, capability and willingness to respond instinctively.

CASE STUDY – Day of disasters

I remember my day-one experience when I became the operational leader of a business unit for the first time. I had to manage two disasters right from the start.

The first disaster was the resignation of the best performing consultant in the business. She told me she had been bullied by my predecessor and had reached the decision that she needed to leave. She planned to go self-employed to preserve her mental health.

This resignation was a big blow to me and to the business as she was such a good colleague and high performer. I said I was very sorry and that I understood her decision. I wished her well with her new venture, although in the moment, I had no idea how we would recover the performance dip that would inevitably follow her departure.

Not long after she left my office, the second disaster arrived in the form of my finance manager shifting uncomfortably in the doorway. I invited him in and asked what was wrong.

He was clearly very stressed as he said there was a major problem. He was so nervous that it took a while for me to understand what he meant. It seemed the business had been failing to deliver on a major contract, leaving us at risk of a financial penalty that was the equivalent of about 25% of the unit's annual turnover.

This was a big deal. Day one was not going brilliantly at that point!

I had no previous experience of this particular situation, but I felt instinctively that the key was to remain calm myself and to calm my colleague so that we could establish all the facts. I started by telling him that he had done the right thing in coming to me and that I was sure we would find a way to resolve the situation. Over the next hour or so, my colleague visibly relaxed as he realised there would be no shouting and no blame being flung about. I was genuinely trying to understand as much about the situation as I possibly could so that we could determine what to do.

Most of the day was spent going through the detail. We invited colleagues in to discuss aspects of the contract and the resources we had in other teams. This enabled us to build a clear understanding of what had gone wrong and what might be available to address the problems. At key points, I would summarise what we knew and would check with others that my understanding was correct so that we could build a shared appreciation of the facts. This made it much easier to move into the 'What if?' phase of our discussion, to start framing the options to address the problems.

In the end, we were successful in putting together a response that involved shifting resources from other work temporarily to recover the position on the key contract, thus mitigating the risk of the financial penalty.

At the end of my first day, I popped in to see my boss. I remember telling him about what had happened and what I had done. He was very encouraging. I will never forget him saying that there was a reason why he had wanted me to take on this new role. He knew not everything was right in the business unit, and he had every confidence in my ability to do the right thing. He said I was right to tell him what had happened and that I should always feel I could come to him any time to talk things over and to get advice.

There were some key takeaways for me from that first day that I now recognise as having shaped my leadership approach over the years:

- There are always bumps in the road and surprises that will arise. The more senior you are, the more problems you will encounter. Accepting this fact helps you stay calm and clear thinking when the unexpected occurs.

- No disaster is ever improved with panic or blame. Although it may not feel instinctive, the more you can dial into a calm setting, the easier you make it for other people firstly to share details of the problem, and secondly to identify solutions.

- All of your attitudes and behaviours as a leader are contagious. If you give way to feelings of overwhelm, anger and panic, you will spread this to others. If you remain calm, curious and clear thinking, you will encourage others to focus on understanding the situation and discovering how it can be resolved. When I spoke with my boss at the end of the day in the example above, I was struck by how my words and actions had mirrored how he had always treated me. Without realising it, I had clearly learned from his example, and this had helped me respond to bad news in a constructive way.

- It is important to keep events in perspective. The more you see them as a problem to be solved, the more likely you are to find solutions. If you label events as a crisis, a catastrophe, a disaster, you are more likely to feel overwhelmed and to sink into a negative emotional cycle. This saps you of the power and confidence you need to take action.

Over the years, I have experienced many events that could be classed as crises, but in the moment, I just saw them as problems that needed to be resolved. Some of these events were quite long lasting.

CASE STUDY – Support through a tough experience

In the early days of my first NHS chair role, I received three whistleblowings alleging serious misconduct by the chief executive and most of the leadership team. These individuals had to be suspended while the allegations were investigated.

For the next two years, I spent an inordinate amount of time managing the subsequent investigation and disciplinary processes, while also making sure the organisation could function. This was challenging as most of the leadership team was suspended for over a year.

This long experience proved to be a tough run, but I had the benefit of great advice and support from colleagues. This made it easier to approach each day with a clear task list of what needed to be done, by whom and by when to manage a complex situation. Communicating daily was a crucial part of keeping everyone informed and focused on seeing the crisis through to a resolution.

CASE STUDY – An unexpected disruption

Sometimes, crisis events arrive unexpectedly without giving you time to reflect or to plan a response. I remember chairing a board meeting that was disrupted by the noisy arrival of a disgruntled former employee and two members of a grieving family who were unhappy with the care their parent had received. These three individuals entered the boardroom about thirty minutes after the meeting had started and proceeded to shout unpleasant accusations and angry questions at various members of the board.

My instinct was to respond calmly. I acknowledged their upset, but I made it clear that disrupting a board meeting was not the appropriate way to raise their concerns. I repeated several times that we were in the middle of a meeting which would continue no matter what. They were welcome to stay as observers, but should not speak; interrupting the meeting would not help to resolve the matters they were raising.

The family members stayed seated and quiet for the most part, but the ex-employee continued to shout. After a while, as she was not getting any attention or response, she gave up.

When the meeting finished, the family members apologised to me and the chief executive for their behaviour and agreed to meet with him to discuss their concerns. The ex-employee remained irate and eventually left the room.

I was glad of the many hours I had spent in the past observing role plays of judicial candidates having to deal with angry and disruptive parties during hearings. I had unconsciously absorbed some key dos and don'ts.

For example, the wrong course of action was to escalate a fraught situation by arguing or issuing threats. This always ended up in the candidate losing control and the whole hearing unravelling. The best-performing candidates remained calm, courteous and authoritative, no matter the provocation.

These observations served me well, and I had a strong instinct on how to handle the situation in the boardroom, although many of my colleagues were decidedly rattled. One member of the company secretarial team was melting with anxiety and suggested several times that security could be called. I refused because I knew this would escalate matters. Asking large men in stab vests to arrive and remove the disruptors from the meeting would only antagonise them and fuel their anger.

Other colleagues looked panicky and fearful as the meeting progressed. I learned after the meeting that some fears were well-founded. The disruptors had, in the preceding months, made various threats to the safety of different staff members. The disgruntled ex-employee had also reported several members of staff maliciously to regulators and professional bodies. I was not aware of these actions at the time. Had I been, I would still have acted in the same way. I remain convinced that the best approach in that situation is to deescalate and defuse tension.

Often, crises are not single events in the moment, but the accumulation of bad decisions over a period of time. Sometimes, these may not have been your bad decisions, but it is still necessary for you to take personal responsibility for handling and resolving the ensuing mess.

CASE STUDY – Own the situation

Soon after I had taken on a chair role with an NHS trust, I was summoned to London by the regulator to account for the organisation's poor financial performance. I had only been in the role for three weeks, so it was clearly not my personal actions that had created the trust's financial difficulties. However, it never entered my mind to do anything other than to own the situation as part of my leadership responsibility. I gave a sincere commitment to work with colleagues to address the situation, and this willingness to take responsibility inspired confidence and bought us some time to find solutions.

When I delved into the history of the trust's finances, it became clear that the current state had been many years in the making and had a number of complex underlying causes. There was no single failure or bad decision that had created the problem. Rather, it was in part the result of operational practices that cumulatively contributed to the build-up of a large financial deficit.

These practices included:

- Operating theatre inefficiency with late starts and cancellations.
- Delayed discharges of medically fit patients, extending their length of stay beyond tariff income levels.
- Poor job planning for clinical staff, affecting productivity and efficient allocation of capacity.
- Frequent use of expensive agency and locum staff to fill rota gaps or to cover staff sickness absence.

The accumulation of these and other issues – such as political insistence that the emergency departments on two sites remained open – had caused a significant financial problem to build over a long period of time. Fortunately, the leadership team was able to work methodically through the data to make improvements.

As a board, we commissioned meaningful analysis to identify the root causes of the financial problem and to prioritise addressing those areas that represented the biggest potential improvements. Finance and operational managers were encouraged to work together to review benchmarking data, to streamline processes and to share learning. Governance processes were reviewed to ensure there was proper reporting, oversight and accountability for the implementation of the financial improvement programme.

Not everything was smooth sailing. I remember a number of colleagues were quite resentful of the regulator's intervention and complained about how unfair it was to be singled out when all NHS trusts were in a similar position. They got mired in long circular discussions about how we were being punished for national budgeting and commissioning decisions outside our control. This was not at all helpful in resolving the situation and took up a lot of time and energy without discernible benefit.

Ultimately, we were able to refocus the efforts of the board more productively. My financially qualified vice chair made a positive contribution to this effort. I found his profound observation that 'weighing the pig doesn't make it any fatter' really helpful in nudging our more recalcitrant colleagues to move beyond analysis and blame and into action.

Personal disasters

We are all human. Experiencing a personal crisis will always spill over into working life.

So many times, I have observed that performance problems or out-of-character behaviours at work are caused by the stress of a personal or a family crisis involving physical health, mental health, relationship breakdown, bereavement or financial pressure. I experienced this myself when my son was ten years old and suffered a life-threatening illness. He was in hospital for endless weeks undergoing daily tests and procedures including eleven surgeries. Throughout this time, I stayed in hospital with him while my daughter stayed with my parents and my husband returned to work.

I recall living in a tiny bubble that was just focused on getting through that day's events: tests, surgeries, vitals checks, intravenous antibiotics and clinicians' visits. It was all-consuming, and there certainly was no headroom for thinking about work or anything else.

I was in the fortunate position of having great family support and running my own business at the time. This meant I could take the necessary time to care for my son. My colleagues and clients were very understanding about my need to reschedule work commitments indefinitely.

Luckily for us, after several months, my son made a full recovery. When he was at last discharged, we could finally breathe a sigh of relief and re-enter normal life.

That time taught me so much. Having gone through such a stressful experience, I developed a huge well of compassion and empathy for others facing up to their own or their family members' ill health.

I know my experience is not unique. Nearly all of my friends, family and colleagues have gone through the mill in dealing with a personal crisis at some stage in their lives.

Having first-hand experience or seeing the impact of a personal crisis on someone close to you can only enhance your ability as a leader to support others compassionately through difficult times. It is worth reviewing whether your policies and processes encourage people to be open when they are struggling. By considering feedback from individuals who have experienced a personal crisis, you can find indications as to whether policies and processes actually deliver support to those who need it.

Dealing with the human aspect of leadership can push us to our limits. The case studies that follow illustrate a time in my career when I felt thoroughly tested.

CASE STUDY – Pressure can get to us all

In one of my early operational leadership roles, the business was facing an externally driven need to restructure. This put immense pressure on the whole management team.

We were charged with reconfiguring the business into a holding company with new subsidiaries and determining where each of the nearly 1,000 employees would end up. Inevitably, there were going to be fewer roles in the new structure with many colleagues at risk of redundancy.

The pressure of this situation was telling on me and others. I have only ever had one shouty argument in my entire career, and it happened during this time.

I remember feeling generally overwhelmed by the responsibility of making decisions that affected others' livelihoods. The spark that triggered the argument was my belief that there had been a breakdown of fair decision making about who had a future role and who was at risk of redundancy. I felt that some staff members were being treated more favourably than others. It was clear that the redundancies were concentrated disproportionately within my business unit, and I was unhappy about having to front a process that appeared to me to be inconsistently applied.

It was far from my finest hour, and I deeply regretted losing it so loudly and so publicly. One of my colleague directors suggested the 'discussion' should be moved from a hallway to his office. I am forever embarrassed that I dismissed his sensible suggestion and continued to vent.

In the end, the situation was resolved and resulted in a fair process. I mention this to show how intense pressure does appalling things to even the most reasonable of people.

CASE STUDY – A devastating tragedy

While we were in the final stages of the restructuring, one of my management team faced an unspeakably horrific personal crisis. On Christmas Day, her sixteen-year-old daughter was murdered. Of course, this was completely devastating for my colleague and her whole family.

I remember going to see her at her home soon after the event. As we sat crying on her sofa, I marvelled that she had the strength to console me and was focused on making me feel better. She told me that she understood I had to make decisions that were right for the business and it would be OK if she did not have a role in the future.

As she was one of the most capable and effective managers in the business unit, there was no prospect of her not having a role, but I was bound by strict instructions not to discuss the new structure at that point. I mentioned to her that all of her colleagues wanted to offer their support and asked if there was anything we could do. She issued an open invitation to the funeral and wake that would be taking place shortly.

On the morning of the funeral, there was an excellent turnout of colleagues wanting to show their support. After the service, a large group of us stood outside the church. I noticed that all eyes were looking to me to offer some leadership and direction. Although I felt totally unprepared for the situation, I decided to trust my gut.

I recognised that there were extreme levels of distress and confusion all around me. Everyone wanted to support our colleague, but they did not want to intrude on the family's grief, and they felt uncomfortable going to the wake.

I made the decision for them. I said no one was going back to work that day. Instead, we would go for a drink together in solidarity with our colleague and her family. After that, everyone would go home for the rest of the day to hug their children and be with their families.

That was such an awful window on to extreme suffering. For me, it was a lesson in just how far the demands on leadership in a crisis can stretch.

CASE STUDY – Being the bearer of bad tidings

As the dust settled on the restructuring, I did have to make a number of staff redundant. My HR director told me that I did not have to meet personally with each individual, and that she and another colleague could conduct the meetings. I appreciated her offer, but felt it was the least I could do to join her in sitting down face-to-face with every individual who was affected and explain the decision that had been reached. I wanted to answer any questions they had and make sure they understood how they would be supported.

Above all, I wanted to embrace the golden rule and ensure they were treated as I would wish to be treated. This meant that I prepared for the meetings by considering if our roles were reversed, how would I want to receive this message?

In the end, the meetings went well. Because there had been constant, honest communication to all the staff, there were no surprises, and those who received bad news felt they had been kept well informed.

I was really moved to be thanked in the meetings for how the whole process had been managed. This was unexpected but much appreciated feedback that really helped me through what I felt was a crisis at that stage of my career.

Although I have had to deliver bad news of this nature on other occasions, I have never lost sight of the significant impact these decisions have on individuals personally and the need to communicate clearly, respectfully and honestly. Experience makes you more confident and better prepared to deliver these difficult decisions, but maintaining a compassionate and humane approach means you always bear in mind the significance of what you are conveying and never become indifferent or blasé.

Big-scale disasters

Over the years, I have been in leadership roles affected by large-scale disasters caused by terror attacks, fire and, of course, the global COVID-19 pandemic.

CASE STUDY – Fire!

In my last chair role, a fire broke out in the plant room on one of our hospital sites. The staff response was exemplary. The chief executive informed me at the outset, and there was good communication throughout the incident with all staff calmly fulfilling their roles.

The smoke from the fire meant the accident and emergency (A&E) department had to be evacuated with patients and ambulances being routed to neighbouring emergency departments for a number of hours. Fortunately, no one was injured and the incident was managed professionally by all involved. The staff followed emergency protocols without fuss, and the senior leaders provided reassuring colleague, partner and media briefings. The organisation received great support from the fire service, the ambulance service and other acute healthcare providers.

Within twenty-four hours, the chief executive provided a comprehensive board briefing on the event and identified what had worked well and what learning could improve the response in future should a similar situation arise. This was a textbook response to an unforeseen event.

The ability to respond so effectively to the fire was, in part, down to the deep learning we had achieved by managing the impact of the COVID-19 pandemic. This had given us all insight into the importance of maintaining calm, undertaking analysis, making decisions and constant communication.

CASE STUDY – A crash course in management

The COVID-19 pandemic presented all NHS trusts with an overwhelming test of leadership and capability. My trust, located in Liverpool, had an over-representation of all the COVID-19 risk factors that resulted in high community transmission rates, severe illness and high mortality.

In March 2020, my colleagues and I reviewed the terrifying forecasts setting out the likely impact of the virus on our population. We were also aware of the horrific events in northern Italy, which we expected would soon be our reality. This glimpse into the future led the board to defer to clinical leaders who were focused on a single purpose: to prepare by quadrupling critical care capacity and allocating theatre and bed capacity according to clinical need.

Although we were scared and facing the unknown, the pandemic stripped away other considerations and was the catalyst for adopting the single-minded focus that was needed at the time. We saw courage and an incredible spirit of team working, support and generosity that were truly inspirational, both within the trust and across the city.

As a leadership team, we applied a crisis management checklist to test that we were acting appropriately and making best use of our resources and governance arrangements. As a result, we limited the call on leaders to attend committee and other meetings and reduced agendas to free up as much time as possible for staff to manage the emergency. We held frequent virtual meetings to share updates and pool knowledge. New daily communications arrangements kept staff and stakeholders informed and updated.

We kept our priorities and our compliance with national guidance under review. For example, when personal protective equipment (PPE) was in short supply, we took the decision to overpay for supplies to keep our staff safe; I recall a discussion where we concluded that as a board, we would prefer to be in trouble for overspending rather than risk staff safety.

The whole experience was a crash course in crisis management for the entire leadership team.

Although the acute phase of the pandemic has receded, the NHS remains in crisis. Prior to the pandemic, it already faced massive challenges, including:

- Increasing demand from a sicker, older population.

- A too small, shrinking and increasingly dissatisfied workforce.

- Lack of investment in prevention, public health and social care.

- Toxic blame cultures and poor relationships between regulators and care providers.

- Shocking quality failures, particularly in maternity and mental-health services.

- Insufficient levels of capital and revenue to provide a safe, modern and efficient infrastructure.

At the time of writing, these demographic, workforce, operational, quality and financial problems are all being made worse by unresolved industrial action with junior doctors, consultants and radiographers continuing to strike. Both sides are increasingly bitter and have resorted to blame and finger-pointing.

This dispute is a stark lesson in how not to resolve a crisis. It is also a cautionary tale about how to reinforce discord, magnify dissatisfaction and fracture relationships within a workforce that has felt taken for granted for years.

Summary

This chapter has described the range of crises that you may experience at work and in your personal life. Some events are long-lasting and some occur in the moment, without warning. Recognising that crises are inevitable is the first step to building the skills needed to manage their arrival. Staying calm, curious and compassionate is the optimal setting for navigating any crisis.

The consistent threads of good practice in a crisis include:

1. Keep calm – succumbing to panic, anger or a temptation to blame, distract or gaslight never helps.

2. Take personal responsibility – even if the crisis is not of your making. If you are a leader, you need to step up and articulate a willingness to understand and address the root of the problem.

3. Start with compassion and empathy – treat others with understanding and apply the golden rule.

4. Embrace your analytical skills – approach every crisis with curiosity and a desire to establish the

facts. Listen carefully. Discuss your analysis with others to develop a shared understanding of the problem. This makes it easier to unlock solutions.

5. Remember, weighing the pig does not make it fatter – avoid getting stuck in analytical mode. Although you may not have perfect information, you must take action. Making the 'least worst' decision is sometimes the best you can do.

6. Communicate constantly – even if you have nothing new to say. Constant communication is reassuring and lets people know the status of the crisis and the action that is planned or underway.

The Firecracker Leader	The Poor Leader
• Stays calm no matter the situation	• Is quick to anger and panic
• Gathers facts and tests understanding	• Analyses only to find someone to blame
• Treats others with compassion	• Dodges responsibility and decision making
• Takes personal responsibility	• Fails to communicate
• Avoids blaming or gaslighting others	• Focuses on self-protection rather than solutions
• Formulates solutions	
• Communicates throughout the crisis	

This chapter has covered the following Firecracker Leadership Framework attributes:

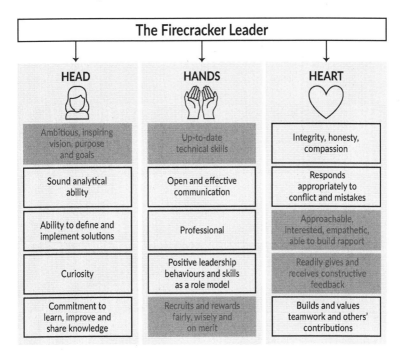

The Firecracker Leader		
HEAD	**HANDS**	**HEART**
Ambitious, inspiring vision, purpose and goals	Up-to-date technical skills	Integrity, honesty, compassion
Sound analytical ability	Open and effective communication	Responds appropriately to conflict and mistakes
Ability to define and implement solutions	Professional	Approachable, interested, empathetic, able to build rapport
Curiosity	Positive leadership behaviours and skills as a role model	Readily gives and receives constructive feedback
Commitment to learn, improve and share knowledge	Recruits and rewards fairly, wisely and on merit	Builds and values teamwork and others' contributions

SIX

How To Survive
The Fishbowl

B eing a leader means living in a fishbowl. Everything you do is visible, observed and remarked upon.

Once you take on a leadership role, you find yourself surrounded by watchful eyes. Your every decision, gesture or comment becomes a topic of interest and conversation.

This level of scrutiny is not always comfortable. The endless attention and gossip can be wearing, and you need to be mindful that everything you do is, in part, defining your organisation's culture. However, life in the fishbowl also presents great opportunities to showcase your leadership skill and lift those around you.

This chapter will help you understand how the best leaders use their visibility as an asset, one that signals positive conduct and shows appreciation for the hard work and achievements of others. There are some cautionary tales, too. These painful examples of floundering under scrutiny are best avoided.

The great leaders described here demonstrate exemplary head, hands, heart qualities. The chapter sets out how you can adopt their good practice by mastering the powerful technique of role modelling. This technique is the secret to thriving – not just surviving – life in the fishbowl.

Learning from royalty

I was privileged to witness exceptional poise and authenticity despite intense scrutiny on a few occasions in my chair role. These occasions provided top drawer demonstrations of great leadership in the full glare of the fishbowl.

CASE STUDY – The art of listening

The first of these occasions was the arrival of Jordan Henderson to the Aintree Hospital site in October 2021. As the captain of Liverpool Football Club, Jordan could most definitely be classed as footballing royalty for the thousands of 'Reds' among staff and patients at the trust. He had also founded the Players Together initiative to raise funds for NHS Charities Together during the pandemic, making his presence on site doubly significant.

As the newly appointed champion for the charity, Jordan arranged for his first visit to be on home turf to Liverpool University Hospitals. He particularly wanted to meet staff who had been directly involved in caring for the thousands of patients affected by the virus. Because of the high community transmission rates at the time, his visit was held outdoors in a garden area that had been created using charitable funds to give staff a place to take a break in a restful, natural environment.

Despite the fact that he was followed around by a BBC camera crew, a number of journalists, photographers and a host of fans, he was incredibly natural and friendly. He put everyone at ease. What struck me most was how interested he was in the staff and how intently he listened to them when they spoke about their experiences over the previous eighteen months.

Liverpool was one of the most affected cities in Europe throughout the pandemic. Coping with an extra wave of the virus and high infection rates, staff at the trust had cared for thousands of COVID-positive inpatients, demonstrating incredible courage and dedication. Some of the staff stories were very poignant with colleagues describing their resulting struggles with post-traumatic stress disorder (PTSD) and the after effects of having had COVID-19 themselves.

Jordan demonstrated amazing empathy and listening skills. He wanted to know how people had fared and how they were coping. He made everyone he spoke with feel that he had all the time in the world and a genuine interest in them. This was an exceptional demonstration of the art of listening, of really embracing the reminder I had received as a child that you have two ears and one mouth, and you are supposed to use them in that proportion.

One of the priorities the board had at the outset of the pandemic was to use charitable funds to create an in-house psychological service to support staff wellbeing. The demands on staff throughout the pandemic were extreme. Witnessing such a high mortality rate among patients who could not have loved ones by their bedside had been very distressing for everyone in the trust, and especially for those individuals providing direct care. As a result, many staff members needed additional support. Jordan's visit provided an opportunity to thank him for raising the charitable funds that enabled this support to become a reality.

I asked him what had motivated him to start the Players Together initiative, and he told me about his relative who worked in the NHS in the North East. Understanding what it was like for frontline staff coping with the pandemic had prompted him to think about what he could do to help. He was completely genuine.

After meeting with staff and conducting media interviews, he stayed for ages posing for photos outside the hospital entrance. He was patient and good-natured about every request. It was incredibly touching to hear him record a phone message for an A&E matron's son who was a Liverpool Football Club super-fan. On the message, Jordan mentioned, 'You're a great lad, and your mum is really proud of you. Just remember, you'll never walk alone.'

One of my board colleagues, who is himself a super-fan, asked what Jordan was really like. I mentioned his amazing listening skills, empathy and kindness, and said, 'When it comes to leadership, he's the real deal.'

CASE STUDY – Leadership royalty

It was a very special day when the Prince and Princess of Wales came to the city in January 2023 to open the new Royal Liverpool Hospital. The preparations were extensive with the hospital and palace teams working closely together for some time to make sure the whole day was planned and organised to go seamlessly.

As the chair of the trust, my role – with my chief executive – was to host the royal couple throughout their long visit and to escort them to various parts of the hospital, introducing them to staff, volunteers and patients. Although the trust was under strict instructions not to broadcast details of their visit, the enormous and overly full media pen opposite the hospital entrance was a bit of a giveaway that something significant was about to happen. As we went to stand by the entrance to await their arrival, we had to fight our way through crowds of staff, patients and members of the public all congregating in the communal area of the ground floor.

As this was their first public engagement since Christmas and since the publication of Prince Harry's book, *Spare*, press interest and presence were even more pronounced than usual.

Looking out at the dozens of film crews and cameras, we had a brief insight into what the royals' fishbowl is like. I can only describe it as extreme, intrusive and unnerving.

Despite this, throughout their long visit, they were unceasingly engaged, charming and delightful to everyone they met. They were exactly the same when off-camera.

When meeting staff, they were totally intent on demonstrating curiosity and concern for their wellbeing. They asked informed questions about job roles, paid careful attention to the answers and asked meaningful follow-up questions, showing their genuine interest was focused on others. With the most flustered and overwhelmed members of staff, they were incredibly kind and reassuring.

On the critical care unit, they met face-to-face many of the same staff with whom Prince William had held a morale-boosting Zoom call in the early stages of the pandemic. They took their time with all the clinical and non-clinical staff on the unit, asking after their health and whether they had managed to get a break over the Christmas holidays. They frequently reminded staff to take time out and to look after themselves. Their compassion was evident.

Elsewhere in the hospital, they met with groups of frontline staff, including many overseas nurses who had moved to Liverpool. They chatted about where colleagues had trained and described their own visits to these countries.

In the public areas of the hospital, they were besieged by attention. Despite this, they posed for endless selfies and chatted good-naturedly. There was some 'boss' Liverpool banter on show as well. Prince William waved to a heavily pregnant member of staff who pointed to her bump, shouting, 'Prince Louis's future wife right here.'

They rightly made a fantastic impression on everyone they met for their warmth and interest.

Their off-camera presence was equally impressive. After a brief private break to have lunch and take a breather, I was bowled over by their courtesy in separately making a point of thanking us for hosting them and for arranging a delicious lunch. When we got back in the lift to continue the visit, there was some good-humoured discussion about just how many Rocky Road bars one of the protection officers had consumed.

Later, after the royal couple had met volunteers and staff providing psychological support to colleagues, we had a conversation about mental health, the board's commitment to investing in an in-house psychological service and the importance of charitable funding to make this happen. Their royal highnesses told me they are patrons of NHS Charities Together and were pleased to hear how the trust had used charitable donations to support staff mental health and wellbeing.

Throughout the day, we saw the deep respect, courtesy and friendly rapport that existed between the royal couple and their team, all of which was generously extended to us in the trust. It was these moments that conveyed that the Prince and Princess of Wales are genuine, authentic and completely at ease in fulfilling their professional responsibilities despite the incomprehensible levels of interest and scrutiny that characterise their fishbowl.

It was disappointing to see that much of the media coverage failed to appreciate the purpose of the royal couple's visit and its significance to the city and its residents. The coverage instead focused on two irrelevant issues.

As they arrived, a random journalist in the media pen had shouted a question about Prince Harry's book. The question was in no way audible to human ears at the distance involved. Nonetheless, the lead on television and in some print media was that the Prince of Wales had refused to answer the question.

Of course, the Princess of Wales is strikingly beautiful and photogenic, but rather than showcasing her warmth and ability to lift everyone's mood, many newspapers confined their comments to her outfit, the cost of her coat and her jewellery.

It struck me as grossly unfair that a couple who had demonstrated such care and interest in others should be marginalised and pigeonholed in this way, but that is clearly part of life in their fishbowl. Their professionalism and ability to be in the moment with others are remarkable, especially given the intense scrutiny that surrounds them.

I was so glad at the end of the visit to have an opportunity to thank the royal couple and to let them know what a tremendous boost to morale their visit had given all of us in the trust. Receiving a goodbye hug from the princess was a highlight that will stay with me always. I do treasure this photo of the four of us taken at the end of the visit, even if the height difference suggests it was 'bring your child to work' day!

For the rest of us, we can be grateful that our daily fishbowl probably does not include forensic analysis of our wardrobe choices or commentary on the state of our family relationships. However, the examples shown by royalty provide useful tips for coping with the attention you do receive in your fishbowl:

1. Take time to prepare. If you are visiting a service or a group of colleagues, do some research to help you ask insightful questions.

2. You have two ears and one mouth. Use them in that proportion.

3. Demonstrate active listening and engaged body language. Eye contact, nodding, smiling and follow-up questions convey a high level of interest and attention.

4. Accept you are being observed and decide to present a friendly, warm, interested face from your fishbowl.

5. Take the initiative by greeting others, making them feel at ease and starting a conversation.

6. Think about your visibility as an opportunity to spread some positivity, appreciation, interest and support to others.

Other winning traits

It is not just royalty and famous sportspeople who know how to demonstrate confidence and leadership in the face of scrutiny. In one of my non-executive chair roles, I was fortunate to work with an excellent chief executive who agreed to step in to support the organisation on a short-term interim basis.

CASE STUDY – Good cop, good cop

On the chief executive's first full day, my colleagues and I were invited to meet in the evening with a large group of senior clinicians. They were deeply unhappy and feeling mutinous over a number of issues, including the previous management team's leadership style.

One director asked the new chief executive if she wanted to be good cop or bad cop at the meeting. She responded, 'Why don't we all be good cops?' I soon learned that this was typical of her mindset and general approach to building relationships.

Although the large group of clinicians provided an initially hostile reception, she displayed all the traits of a good cop and a great leader. She explained that she was new, she realised there was a mood of discontent and she was there to listen and understand. She invited all those who wished to speak to do so openly and without judgement.

As the meeting progressed, the group warmed to her genuine approach and willingness to listen attentively. She went on to receive good support from the clinical body. No doubt this was down to her exceptional ability, but setting the tone at that meeting in the face of an icy reception was a crucial first step.

CASE STUDY – Showing vulnerability

On another occasion, an interim chief executive I appointed made a positive first impression when he spoke in detail at an event for the organisation's senior leaders. The scheduling was helpful in that the long-planned event was due to take place just a few days after his arrival. It was a good opportunity for him to share the priorities the board had set and to describe how he would seek to work within the organisation.

He gave a detailed presentation on these points and described his leadership experience and impressive track record in similar roles. He also referenced his own values and beliefs. These emphasised the importance of respect, deferring to clinical expertise and creating an environment where colleagues felt valued, committed and willing to give discretionary effort in the quest for improvement. He asked for others to help and support him in meeting the improvement priorities for the organisation.

This was all good stuff, but what really stood out for me were two slides he showed at the end of the presentation to describe how he was feeling about taking on the challenge of the interim role. The first slide contained an image of a shirtless Rambo, complete with bandoliers of bullets across his chest and a smattering of jungle camouflage greasepaint. The caption read, 'How it appears'. The second slide displayed an image of a wailing tear-stained baby with the caption, 'How it feels'.

His confidence to show vulnerability was disarming and a masterstroke. In showing his human side to the fishbowl, he immediately built rapport and understanding among judgemental critics.

My most recent chief executive was appointed because of his outstanding ability to analyse and solve problems and his compassionate leadership style. He exemplifies head, hands, heart leadership skill.

CASE STUDY – Safety concerns

Early on in this chief executive's role, there was a specific incident that really showcased his authenticity and leadership skills.

A woman was brutally attacked in one of the car parks used by staff. This was an event that was very distressing and concerning for all and was covered in detail by local and social media.

The attack triggered a host of anxieties and concerns from staff, which poured forth during an online team briefing event. The concerns related to poor safety arrangements in the car park, which was owned and operated by a private company, and more generally to not feeling safe or cared for at work.

Despite only being in post for a brief time, the new chief executive's response was exemplary. He listened carefully and signalled ownership of the concerns. He urged anyone who wished to raise anything to come forward so he could be sure he had a full understanding.

Having gained a complete picture, which included, for example, problems like broken security locks as well as a sense of frustration at receiving no response after raising concerns in the past, he proposed and implemented a range of improvements. These included putting closed circuit television (CCTV) cameras in place which would be monitored by trust security staff, making personal safety equipment available to all and addressing cultural gaps to improve psychological safety. With this approach, he demonstrated how to lead with integrity, a solution focus and empathy under scrutiny.

As part of my judge-appointing role, I get the opportunity to observe a court or tribunal before assessing the applications of aspiring judges. These observations are a great chance to see the required judicial skills in action and always prove to be fantastically interesting and educational.

On the subject of surviving the fishbowl, one of these visits stands out in my memory.

CASE STUDY – A well-liked judge

I was observing a significant fraud trial in Manchester and was invited by the judge to sit next to him on the bench. On that day, a key witness was being cross-examined. There were reams of documents and some very technical aspects of law and procedure being explored. At times, the judge would intervene with a question when he sought to clarify an issue.

This was such an interesting window on a judge's fishbowl where every word is recorded and every gesture is scrutinised by both sides to gauge what the judge is thinking. As a vastly experienced and capable judge, my host demonstrated all the attention and independent authority required of the role. At that stage of the trial, it was his job to make sure both sides had an opportunity to present and examine all relevant evidence so that he could reach fair and reasoned decisions on the facts.

When the trial paused for a lunch break, the judge showed me out through the private door behind the bench. As the door closed, he exclaimed, 'Did you hear *that*?' He then explained the significance of the witness's answers to the final questions.

Although the witness had admitted to falsifying records, the judge's demeanour had not changed in court. Despite the emergence of this significant fact, he remained independent, attentive and open-minded until all the evidence was presented and examined.

After a quick sandwich, the judge gave me a tour of the building and introduced me to his clerk and other court staff. I was struck by the great respect and affection his colleagues had for him. In court, he exhibited a judicial presence of great gravitas, independence and wisdom. Behind the scenes, he was also a generous and well-liked colleague with a good sense of fun.

One of the court staff pointed to a bookshelf groaning with tubs and bars of chocolate which the judge had provided for others, and then to a small pile of chocolate bars on a separate shelf, saying, 'That's the judge's chocolate.' As it was the only kind he liked, she made sure there was a separate supply available just for him.

The judge had demonstrated an important balancing act in surviving the fishbowl: maintaining authority and commanding respect while being friendly and approachable.

At the other end of the spectrum

If royalty and others have provided some good practice lessons, I have also observed some real clangers in the face of public attention and scrutiny. In my chair roles, I have hosted a fair few visits from government ministers. There has certainly been a high level of churn in ministerial office in recent times.

CASE STUDY – Thank you for nothing

A minister informed us he would be visiting the trust I was chairing. He was speaking at a conference nearby and wanted to generate some positive PR about... well anything, but he specifically chose 'innovation' as his hook.

The chief medical officer and I were on duty to escort him first to see the theatre where robotic surgery was being undertaken, then throughout the hospital site and on to a clinical sciences building where he would also conduct television and radio interviews. He was with us for a couple of hours, but it felt much longer. Never have I had to work so hard to hold a conversation with anyone. The man had absolutely no chat! I was astonished that he had no questions and never asked about anything happening in the organisation. I had to fill in the silences and was close to exhausting my list of facts and topics that I thought he would find interesting or helpful to know.

He did ask one question of a surgeon. He sought agreement that the advent of robotic surgery would reduce waiting times for elective patients, clearing the backlog quickly. As the surgical team he met was using the robot to operate on complex gastrointestinal tumours, the answer was no. His face fell at this news. He was clearly hoping a yes would give him a helpful sound bite.

It was only when the cameras were on that he became animated. Some of his attempts to look benevolent and masterful were wretched failures. There was one moment where he spotted a group of people in blue polo shirts waiting by a lift that was particularly cringe-inducing. As the cameras were whirring, he made a beeline for a young man in the centre of the group and stuck his hand out with an oozing declaration of, 'Thank you so much for all you are doing.'

The baffled young man shook his hand, whereupon a woman in the group asked, 'Eh, who's he?'

The young man in receipt of the handshake replied, 'I've no idea, and I don't know why he's thanking us when it's our first day and we are on our induction tour.'

Here are three other examples of getting it wrong from the fishbowl: being mean, selfish or menacing.

CASE STUDY – Being mean to the admin

I was once chairing a panel to appoint a resident judge for a city. The panel included the then senior presiding judge, reflecting the significance of the role and its demanding responsibilities, such as hearing the most serious criminal cases, providing leadership and support to other judges, and serving as the public face of the judiciary in the community.

There were two short-listed candidates who were both experienced and capable judges. On paper, one seemed to be particularly accomplished. He had risen quickly through judicial ranks and had received glowing references.

However, on the day, he had not really prepared well for the interview and did not provide compelling evidence of his abilities. It was almost as if he thought it was beneath him to have to answer the panel's questions. He was the 'Don't you know who I am?' type of candidate who thinks they are entitled to automatic appointment. As a panel, we agreed unanimously that the other candidate should be recommended for appointment.

When we were finishing for the day, the front-of-house colleague who had been escorting the candidates throughout the process came to say goodbye. I thanked her for her help and asked her if everything had gone OK. She said there had been highs and lows, and volunteered some thoughts.

Of the candidate who was recommended for appointment, she said, 'He was so nice and kind. He asked me all about my role. I hope he gets the job.' Of the seemingly more able candidate, she said, 'He was really rude and treated me like a servant.'

The unsuccessful candidate had clearly had a bad day on all counts, but this was a reminder of how important it is to treat everyone with respect and courtesy, no matter your role, their role or the situation.

An indicator of a great leader is the consistent demonstration of respect and courtesy to all. Adopting this practice shows your true colours and makes people feel better for having been in your company.

CASE STUDY – Tone-deaf selfishness

One year, I was invited to attend a Christmas party for the volunteers. This was an event designed to thank volunteers for giving their time and effort so generously to support patients and the work of the trust.

On this particular occasion, I was sitting next to another director on a table with six volunteers. There were at least 100 volunteers attending, and it was a fun night with a nice meal, a raffle and a band.

While the meal was coming to an end, every diner was asked if they wished to buy raffle tickets. The prizes that had been donated were spread out over a large table, and there was an air of expectation around the room as the winning numbers were drawn.

My colleague had an amazing lucky streak that night. She had purposely purchased a strip of tickets from each of the different coloured books that were available and, no word of exaggeration, she had the winning ticket seven times.

There is an unwritten rule that if you are a leader in an organisation, you should definitely buy tickets for raffles, but you should not accept the prize. My inclination has always been that if you are fortunate enough to be in a well-paid role, which every board member is, you should demonstrate some sensitivity and awareness about your position in relation to others and decline the prize. That is just my view, though, and I would not have judged had my colleague won once or maybe even twice.

By the seventh time she went up to choose from the prizes, there was an uncomfortable atmosphere and some audible mumbling, which in Britain indicates seething outrage. This was a real failure to read the room and understand the unspoken messages that were being communicated.

Those who had donated prizes clearly thought they were providing nice items to recognise the contribution of unpaid volunteers. They had not been asked to reward highly paid members of the board who were in a position of relative financial advantage. In accepting the prizes, my colleague was either unaware or unconcerned about what message her actions were sending.

CASE STUDY – The mendacious chair whisperer

One organisation that I chaired faced some significant challenges in terms of staff recruitment and retention, and addressing these problems was a priority for the board. Nonetheless, I was surprised to receive an oddly apologetic email from a senior manager who asked if he and another colleague could please meet with me to go through their draft recruitment and retention strategy and the actions they were proposing.

The answer from me was, 'Yes, of course'. I was keen to offer any help and support I could and was interested to learn their thoughts on solutions that could help improve the situation.

On the day, I was baffled by how nervous and uncomfortable they both seemed. They were exhibiting what could only be described as acute fear. I tried my best to make them feel at ease and gave them honest, appreciative and constructive feedback on the work they had done.

Although they were more relaxed at the end of the meeting than the beginning, I really was puzzled about why they were so scared. I'm not physically imposing, for sure, and I could not think of any behaviour I had demonstrated that would make them fear me.

Another colleague had told me that their boss used a manipulative, task-based, 'just f**king do it' style of management. She thought people only responded to instructions coming from on high, and she wanted to be seen as having inner circle access that made her an authoritative mouthpiece representing decision makers.

I decided to ask why the two colleagues had seemed so afraid to meet me, and the answer was horrible. Apparently, they had been told by their boss, 'The chair is raging. She blames you for the retention problems. You better show some progress or she said she is going to sack you.'

I was really shocked at the blatant lying and the threats made by a senior professional who was meant to be the keeper of the organisation's values. Once I heard this, I understood why the two colleagues had been so fearful. What a dreadful abuse of power.

Terrorising your team, ruling by bullying and invoking the power of others: these are truly appalling leadership approaches. This lowest common denominator behaviour creates fear, not respect, and is no way to navigate the fishbowl.

CASE STUDY – There is always room for improvement

I had the good fortune to work with an accomplished chief executive, and it was a real pleasure to read all the positive comments about them captured in a 360-degree survey as part of an annual appraisal. The overall picture was a well-deserved endorsement of expert leadership.

Amid all the comments relating to excellent qualities, there were a few that indicated, at times, less attention to the nuances of life in the fishbowl than was necessary. The comments focused on two linked issues.

The first issue concerned personal impact on others. The comments described the chief executive as powerful, persuasive, commanding, inspiring belief, but there were also numerous requests to receive personalised feedback.

For really capable leaders, the fishbowl can magnify their power and create a desire to know 'what they really think of me' in others. The comments relating to this issue were a backhanded compliment, indicating the leader was held in high regard and followers wanted to receive their approval.

The second issue concerned comments the chief executive had made that were critical or dismissive of colleagues or peers in other organisations. The comments that highlighted this issue were code for: if you are being critical of others who are not in the room, what do you really think and say about me when

I am not here? Again, this is a reflection of the desire to receive approval, not criticism, from a leader who is seen as powerful and capable.

If your followers respect you, they will also want to secure your good opinion. For them, not knowing what you really think creates anxiety. In these circumstances, taking the time to provide honest, meaningful feedback, telling them what you think, is the best way to dispel self-doubt and boost confidence in others.

As a general rule, it is never a good look to criticise others in public. This makes you appear petty, and it plants seeds with colleagues that you are the type of person who takes shots at people behind their backs. It does not take your followers long to fear that they might be the next target of your criticism.

Role modelling

The best way to survive the fishbowl is to understand and master the power of role modelling. In the introduction, when I suggested that it would be easy for you to think of good and poor leaders you have known, it was because I understand just how significant these examples are and how firmly they have become embedded in your memory and your subconscious.

All of us practise role modelling or copying on an unconscious level. This is why prevailing behaviours become so easily entrenched and are so difficult to change. As humans, we unconsciously tune into and absorb 'the way things are done around here', which is the standard definition of organisational culture. We are programmed to copy the patterns of behaviour we perceive in others, particularly leaders, because we understand from their example what is expected, appropriate and rewarded.

This exceptionally powerful process occurs all the time. It can be immensely frustrating to try to change culture because of how strongly this unconscious learning takes hold.

When there is a difference between what is said and what is done, we are physiologically wired to copy what is done and to disregard what is said. This unconscious copying reinforces the existing culture and status quo. Even if there are strategies, posters, videos, emails, whiteboards and screensavers describing the way things should be, leaders in organisations struggle to make change happen if there is dissonance between the desired state and what is actually practised.

To break this cycle, the first step is to develop your conscious understanding of the power of role modelling. When it comes to your own conduct and behaviour, commit consciously to being a role model worthy of emulation. This means being selective about the behaviours you display in the full knowledge that you are in the fishbowl and that others will observe, judge and copy what you do.

Ralph Waldo Emerson is credited with saying, 'What you do speaks so loudly, I can't hear what you say.' This apt phrase has stuck with me. In short, actions always speak louder than words.

I would add: know that as a leader, others will do as you do. They will copy your actions, not what you say you value, admire or wish to see.

In Chapter 5, I described dealing with a day-one crisis and realising that my response had mirrored the way my boss treated me. I had such respect for his ability that when faced with an unfamiliar problem, I instinctively and unconsciously behaved as I had observed him behave in the past.

This was a game-changing realisation for me. From that point on, I shifted my awareness to observe, identify and copy the good practice in others that I wanted to replicate. I also noted the terrible practice that made me flinch and determined that I would not make that kind of behaviour part of my own conduct. This was really helpful every time I took on a new role or a new challenge.

Throughout my career, I have had the good fortune of witnessing great leadership in others. Making these observations has helped me navigate my own roles with confidence.

All of us are first-timers at some stage of our career. It is at these moments that you can help yourself by relying on the positive examples that have been set for you in the past. Choose selectively and consciously the approaches that you admire in others. This will serve you well, even when you are faced with the unknown.

However, it is important that you internalise and don't plagiarise! This means you should observe and identify good practice, and then think about how you can make this your own.

Ask yourself, 'How can I demonstrate the behaviour I admire in my own way, with my own personality and my own voice?' Taking this thoughtful approach will make the behaviours authentic to you. Your example will therefore resonate convincingly and genuinely from your fishbowl to your audience.

Gather feedback

The best way to establish whether you are navigating the fishbowl effectively is to ask. You can use a range of methods to gather feedback on your performance.

The more structured methods include:

- Appraisal
- 360-degree feedback surveys

- Professional revalidation

- Staff surveys

- Customer surveys

- Pulse check surveys

- Virtual / online consultations

- Exit interviews

- Inspection reports

- Stakeholder surveys

Sometimes having a coffee with others in a small group can create a relaxed environment where it is appropriate to discuss the findings from the sources of feedback available to you. Asking colleagues you trust to tell you the truth is a valuable way to check and validate feedback.

Keep an open mind and a willingness to understand when you are hearing or reading through these results. You may need to boost your patience and serenity levels in advance to avoid giving way to reactions of defensiveness or exasperation!

Friendly, not friends

A final quick word of advice on surviving the fishbowl. Developing leaders often make the mistake of blending friendship and leadership. This is a bad error to make. So many times, I have seen leaders come to grief when they have had to address a difficult performance issue or make a difficult decision that affects colleagues who are also friends.

The gossip that surrounds the fishbowl is often concerned with allegations of nepotism. Leaders who confuse leadership with friendship leave themselves seriously exposed.

Almost without exception, I have liked all the colleagues I have been fortunate to work with over the years. I have appreciated all their fine qualities, valued their contributions and enjoyed their company. However, I have always drawn a line between the personal and the professional when I have been in a leadership role. Not everyone agrees with me, but I think this is the smartest choice when you are a leader and need to be objective about others' work performance.

Having to make difficult decisions that affect others' livelihoods is hard enough without adding in the complicating factor of the bonds of friendship. My mantra has always been to be friendly, but not friends. This means you can still be approachable, supportive, warm, compassionate and an all-round good person. And, you avoid the conflict of interest that comes when the right course of action for a leader differs to the right course of action for a friend.

Summary

This chapter has described how to survive in the leadership fishbowl. Being a leader makes you a figure of constant interest for colleagues and critics who watch your every move.

Borrow communication tips from royalty, be a good cop and show your vulnerability when the time is right. Use the power of role modelling to become a leader worthy of following. Avoid false and petty behaviours that rob you of your integrity, authenticity and authority. Seek feedback on how well you are navigating the rigours of the fishbowl.

The Firecracker Leader	The Poor Leader
• Recognises that being always on show is an opportunity to role model positive behaviours	• Fails to recognise the fishbowl is perpetual
• Uses their visibility to focus on others	• Lacks curiosity or interest in others
• Listens with curiosity, warmth and empathy	• Talks more than listens
• Uses two ears and one mouth in proportion	• Succumbs to insincere, selfish or bullying conduct
• Provides honest, constructive feedback	• Refuses to demonstrate sensitivity or vulnerability
• Welcomes feedback from others	• Criticises others publicly
• Avoids nepotism and conflicts of interest	• Does not recognise the risk of merging leadership and friendship

This chapter has covered the following Firecracker Leadership Framework attributes:

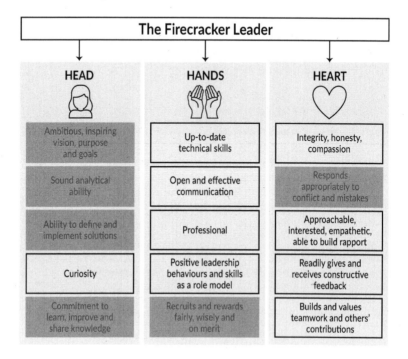

The Firecracker Leader

HEAD	HANDS	HEART
Ambitious, inspiring vision, purpose and goals	Up-to-date technical skills	Integrity, honesty, compassion
Sound analytical ability	Open and effective communication	Responds appropriately to conflict and mistakes
Ability to define and implement solutions	Professional	Approachable, interested, empathetic, able to build rapport
Curiosity	Positive leadership behaviours and skills as a role model	Readily gives and receives constructive feedback
Commitment to learn, improve and share knowledge	Recruits and rewards fairly, wisely and on merit	Builds and values teamwork and others' contributions

SEVEN

How To Stay Resilient

Great leaders understand that resilience – the ability to persevere no matter what – must be nurtured and protected. Knowing what gives you energy, motivation, fuel in the tank is essential. This is what enables you to face adversity or, paradoxically, to avoid feeling depleted after a big win.

You owe it to yourself to make sure you know what adds credit to your resilience bank and what constitutes a withdrawal. You need to keep topping up your resilience balance if you are to avoid burnout and remain fit to stay in the game for the long term.

Your resilience balance can be topped up by:

- Embracing good habits – programming yourself to cope with adversity

- Goal setting – goals create energy
- Investing in you – your physical, mental and emotional health
- Spending quality time with inspirational ideas and people – your resilience boosters
- Laughing – laughter is the best medicine

Programme yourself to cope with adversity

Investing in the habits that build resilience will repay you at those times of crisis or adversity that are inevitable in your life as a leader.

I had a surprising knock out of the blue when I was told that my reappointment to a second term in my chair role was being blocked by the Secretary of State for Health and Social Care 'for political reasons'. That was the only explanation I received.

The person who relayed this message said, 'This is unjust and unfair.' Although we could both agree on that, it was clear to me that as a decision had been made without discussion or explanation, it would be futile to attempt to argue it.

This kind of nonsense happens all the time to people in leadership roles, particularly those roles that are subject to political interference. It does not matter how strong your track record has been, what you have achieved, what your performance appraisals say or how much your colleagues value you, your tenure will at times be affected by political decision making that has nothing to do with your ability.

Having established that there are no grounds to challenge the decision, a leader in this situation has two choices:

- Option A: speak out loudly and often about the unjust and unfair error that has been made.

- Option B: determine that acceptance is in the best interests of you, the organisation and the people you serve.

In my experience, Option A may provide a short-term catharsis, but it is highly unlikely to result in a changed decision, and it always damages your reputation and others' headspace. Option B may feel unpalatable in the short term, but again, in my experience, it is the mature, professional and positive course. Option B is the manifestation of resilience.

I was once terribly disappointed not to be chosen for a more senior role in an organisation, and I was aggrieved about the appointment process and the conduct of the person who had chaired the panel. I made the mistake of choosing Option A. After initially feeling vindicated, I then found that sustaining righteous indignation was just exhausting. Maintaining a level of outrage merely kept disappointment and anger alive. This prevented me from moving forward with life, and unhappily, it seemed to be the defining feature of my interactions with all my colleagues. Having to relive an unhappy event constantly is draining and a blocker to progress.

When I received the bad news described above, it never entered my head to choose Option A again. Once I had explored with colleagues whether the decision was contestable, I was clear that Option B was the only viable course of action.

Above all, I was driven by acting in the best interests of the organisation and the population we served. My responsibility as a leader in public office was to uphold the Nolan Principles[18] and to separate my personal feelings of disgust from my professional obligations.

Of course, I was angered by the decision, and I was enormously grateful for the support of my colleagues who felt first incredulous, and then outraged when they heard the news. However, having been in a similar situation in the past, and having witnessed many other leaders' responses, I knew that stoking everyone's anger would only damage relationships with regulators and serve as a distraction from the real purpose of the organisation.

The situation called for a responsible, mature, professional demonstration of leadership and personal

HOW TO STAY RESILIENT

resilience. Although I appreciated my colleagues' fury at the decision and their concern for me on a personal level, I was able to persuade them that acceptance was the right response. I urged them to focus all their energies on taking the organisation forward and was able to reassure them that I would genuinely be fine. I saw the situation as an opportunity for me to decide my next steps positively, particularly having the time to write this book!

All the resilience habits I had developed over the years, particularly in leading through the pandemic, gave me unshakeable confidence that I was doing the right thing. I possessed the clarity of mind to see the truth of Napoleon Hill's wise words, 'Every adversity, every failure, every heartache carries with it the seed of an equal or greater benefit.'[19]

Goals create energy

At the heart of every book on success is the importance of goal setting. Setting goals is the process by which you give meaning and direction to your life. A by-product of having clearly defined goals is a massive boost to personal resilience.

Not only do goals pull you towards your purpose, they give you the personal armour you need to withstand setbacks, criticism and adversity. If you know where you are going, what you are seeking to achieve and why, you become more motivated and unstoppable. If you are not so sure about your purpose or aspirations, you will be much more susceptible to being knocked off course by life events and others' opinions.

Many leaders understand the relevance of setting organisational purpose and goals (as described in Chapter 2). Only the best leaders understand that having aligned personal goals is fundamental to maintaining their own resilience and ability to be effective at work.

There are so many brilliant books on goals. Authors like Napoleon Hill, Zig Ziglar, Jim Rohn, Brian Tracy, Les Brown and Tony Robbins have explained the importance of goals and how to set them. You can find titles by these authors recommended in the 'Further Reading' page.

The most important thing is to give this process the time and energy it requires to be meaningful. In writing down your goals, setting a timescale for their achievement and committing to take action, you will unlock improved levels of motivation and resilience.

When you are driven by goals, particularly those that benefit more people than just yourself, it is the equivalent of inoculating yourself against criticism or praise. For example, when I was chairing an organisation that was struggling to meet a number of operational targets, I recognised that growing my knowledge of the science of performance improvement would help me make better decisions. I set a goal to master this knowledge.

Setting that goal unlocked access to internal and external expertise that I was previously unaware of and led to me specifying workshop content that was educational and motivational. Going on visits to see how other organisations had applied performance improvement methods helped me develop my knowledge. Achieving this goal enabled me to contribute to designing and monitoring a performance improvement strategy that created notable results.

I have set personal goals to develop my knowledge of digital and other technological developments to make me more effective in my leadership roles. I have found that aligning my personal goals to the organisation's goals enables me to ask better questions, to understand investment requirements and to make more informed decisions.

Having personal goals around fitness and exercise has helped me develop the physical stamina and mental resilience needed to work in a pressured environment. Sometimes this is good fun, too. I set a goal to run in the Scouse 5k to raise money for a breast cancer charity. On this occasion, the whole family joined in to share in a fantastic experience that was good for our health and successful in raising a tidy sum for a great cause.

Investing in you

Maintaining your physical, mental and emotional health is key to sustaining your resilience. This means eating well, moving well, thinking well and taking breaks.

Eating well

It is surprising how little emphasis there is in the medical education curriculum on nutrition, given its importance to maintaining good health and preventing illness. Although we all know what we should do, we do not always put this knowledge into practice. The quote from the late motivational speaker and author Stephen Covey, 'To know and not to do is really not to know', is apposite.[20]

CASE STUDY – From baguette to wellness champion

About seven months into the pandemic, I hit a wall. The trust that I was chairing had experienced an additional wave of COVID-19, and the pressures and stress of the situation were just immense.

I found it difficult not to be able to see family during this time. Unbelievably, my mother had had a stroke during our weekly family Zoom call. It was such an out-of-body experience to be watching on a laptop 3,000 miles away the ambulance crew arrive and take her to hospital. Fortunately, she was and is fine, but it was very stressful not being able to be there physically with her and my father when she was unwell.

My husband and I found not seeing our children especially wearing. We had finally arranged a weekend visit in late October and were so disappointed when the lockdown rules changed the night before, and we could not travel.

As 2020 was drawing to a close, I felt very low, and there was little cheer as Christmas was approaching. Normally in early December, the board would visit and distribute boxes of chocolates to all departments and teams, but that year, I sat with two colleagues in a conference room, wearing face masks and receiving one individual at a time, who would say hello, sanitise their hands, have a brief chat and pick up the chocolates to take back to their teams.

One of my colleagues noted that so many staff looked weary and low in energy and had gained weight during the lockdown. She suggested we would need to look at introducing some new wellbeing support.

While we were sitting in the conference room,
I received two end-of-year messages that really chimed
with her observation. The first one was from a fitness
app on my phone, which showed that throughout the
stressful month of November, I had averaged about 300
steps a day (compared to my normal 7,000–10,000).
The second message was from Marks & Spencer, my
favourite supermarket, informing me that I was twelfth
on the local leader board for baguette purchases that
year. My colleague received a similar update and
announced that she was third for quiche buying.

Although we laughed about it at the time, and I joked
that I wanted to be known as 'Twelfth for Baguettes',
this data gave me a real insight. I recognised that as
I felt more stressed at work and upset about missing
family, I had fallen into a spiral of inactivity, eating
rubbish food, drinking more and sleeping poorly. It was
clear that a typical day in November involved walking
from my bedroom to my desk where I sat on Teams calls
all day, followed by walking to the sofa where I would
consume baguettes and drink wine until bedtime!

This cycle was no good at all, and I resolved to
look after my health better as I could really feel my
resilience depleting.

Moving well

I was sceptical when my husband told me he had
booked us and our daughter for a hot yoga class, but
it proved to be my salvation. I had only been to one
yoga class years before, and I had not enjoyed it. My
recollection of that class was of lying inert on a mat

under a blanket and being encouraged to breathe in and out.

Hot yoga is completely different. We were so fortunate to find Hot Buddha, an amazing studio nearby with wonderful teachers and friendly, welcoming members. The classes are challenging, but so enjoyable and a complete boon to body, mind and spirit. I am still a beginner, but also a determined trier. It is thrilling to find that some days, I am able to achieve a pose that has been eluding me.

Throughout the pandemic, it was such a relief to be told to leave the day's to-do list at the door and just spend an hour moving and breathing. It was like having permission to take a break from grim reality and hit the reset button. I would highly recommend yoga to anyone, regardless of age, fitness or flexibility.

Of course, there are many different types of exercise, and I suggest you find one you like and stick with it. Giving yourself an hour of a quiet mind, freedom from distraction and time to reflect on what you are grateful for is a gift that boosts your resilience and ability to cope.

Thinking well

Many people swear by meditation as the ideal way to build and sustain high levels of resilience, and there are numerous books, apps and courses on the subject. Personal development systems regularly include the elements of goal setting, visualisation and affirmation introduced by Napoleon Hill in *Think and Grow Rich*.[21] Systems that are well established and well regarded include The Silva Method,[22] The Pacific Institute[23] and Tony Robbins's events and training.[24] Numerous programmes available on Mindvalley.com provide additional valuable options.

At its heart, each of these systems emphasises the importance of entering a relaxed state and visualising and affirming your goals as if they are already achieved. Daily practice creates the belief you need to keep going, no matter what difficulties come your way.

Some affirmations that really help with building resilience include:

- Every day in every way, I am getting better, better and better.

- Every day the universe gives me a lesson to make me a better person.

- I turn problems that come my way into a project.

- I solve all problems easily and effortlessly.

- I am resilient and cope with whatever comes my way.

The key is to find an approach that works for you in building your resilience and to make it part of your routine.

Take regular breaks

To sustain your resilience, you need to switch off and get away regularly. Resting and enjoying a change of scenery is restorative and gives you a valuable sense of perspective.

You should not feel guilty about taking time off. It is essential to recharge your batteries if you are to avoid burnout. Think about what is most restorative for you. Apart from major holidays, small breaks of a few days can be just what you need to top up your resilience.

For me, going to Scotland with family and friends is the perfect way to relax and refresh my levels of vim and vigour. A few days in the company of loved ones with beautiful scenery, lovely beaches and the fresh air of the Highlands always works wonders.

Resilience boosters

Spending quality time with inspirational ideas and people always enhances personal resilience. There are so many options to top up your inspiration levels:

- Reading books and articles

- Listening to podcasts

- Watching videos

- Attending virtual or in-person workshops and seminars

Again, whatever medium you prefer, routinely accessing new ideas and information will give you motivation and inspiration that, in turn, enhance your resilience.

Some of the key benefits of workshops and seminars are that there are fewer distractions and you spend time with like-minded people who share your interests. I regularly attend online and in-person events even on subjects that are familiar to me. There is always something new to learn. Investing time in personal development is never wasted, and meeting other people brings an opportunity to learn something useful from their experience.

Demonstrating your commitment to learning is an excellent way to lead by example. No matter how accomplished you are, you will need to refresh your knowledge and keep your technical skills up to date. If you had to have an operation, would you choose the surgeon who practises every day or the one who tells you they aced their exams fifteen years ago so you can have every confidence you are in good hands?

Use positive self-talk

A fundamental part of programming yourself to cope with whatever comes at you is mastering your self-talk. Self-talk is the voice inside your head that never switches off.

I was surprised during an appraisal meeting to hear from an experienced colleague that he had not heard the term 'self-talk' before. We were discussing how to develop more confidence, and I had asked him about the quality of his self-talk.

He was unaware that his self-talk was undermining his ability to express himself confidently in his role. I asked him what the voice inside his head was saying to him when he was speaking in public. Unfortunately, it was filling him with doubt about his competence and making him second-guess his credibility.

I shared with him the good news. All of us can programme our self-talk. Even if you are not aware of it, you are programming that voice all the time through your thoughts and beliefs about yourself.

What you feed your mind determines the content of your self-talk. If you repeat things that are negative and undermining, your self-talk will remind you of your weaknesses, doubts and failings. If you repeat things that are positive, your self-talk will remind you that you are a confident, capable, resilient leader who has good judgement, good intentions and good instincts.

Self-talk is a by-product of your beliefs, an echo of whatever you believe about yourself. It is therefore entirely trainable through repetition of messages that you believe. It is your choice to select the input, so help yourself and choose constructive content. Affirm these beliefs in the present tense as often as possible so that they become locked into your system.

Choose wisely

As a leader, you do need to be careful about who you take advice from and who you trust to take into your confidence. As Jim Rohn says, 'You are the average of the five people you spend the most time with.'[25]

Leadership can be a lonely place, but it is important for your resilience that you have access to advice and inspirational new ideas. Many leaders find it helpful to have a coach or a mentor who can help them grow and think differently about problems, but choose wisely.

Your colleagues, friends and family may be great company and supportive, lovely people. However, when it comes to taking advice or navigating leadership problems, they cannot help you if they have not been where you are or have not done what you seek to accomplish. Only take advice from someone who has achieved what you wish to achieve, has navigated the kinds of challenges you face and has demonstrated the values and qualities that you admire.

In my experience, the busiest and most successful people also tend to be the most generous in giving time to help others succeed. Consider who might be best placed to serve as your mentor and have the courage to ask them to help you. If you choose well, you will most likely be pleasantly surprised at the response you receive.

If you have not got access to a suitable mentor, you might try the method of forming a virtual master-mind group as described by Napoleon Hill.[26] He would hold imaginary meetings with business leaders to seek their guidance.

Laughter is the best medicine

Holding a leadership role is a serious responsibility. Some roles involve working in high-risk environments where decisions have serious consequences for the wellbeing and lives of others. Working in these environments requires great resilience *and* the ability to avoid becoming oppressed by the weight of the responsibilities you carry.

The best way to cope is to laugh more. According to the highly regarded Mayo Clinic, laughter truly is the best medicine.[27]

The Mayo Clinic research shows that laughter creates positive effects on your mental and physical health. The short- and long-term benefits of laughing include:

- Less stress as your heart rate and blood pressure decrease

- Less tension as your muscles relax and circulation improves

- More endorphins released by your brain, making you feel relaxed and happy

- A stronger immune system through the release of neuropeptides that fight stress and illness

- Pain relief

- More connection with others

- Less stress, depression and anxiety, making you feel happier

Laughing feels good and puts you on a sustainable, resilient path.

CASE STUDY – Grand national runner kidnapped

I believe work – even in the most serious, high-pressured environments – is supposed to be enjoyable and fun.

Many years ago, I was leading a business that was lucky to employ a fantastic sales manager. He was creative in finding ways to motivate his team. One of his ideas was to incentivise colleagues by rewarding the person who achieved the most sales within a promotional period. To provide a visual way of tracking progress, he built a Grand National racecourse in the office, complete with toy horses, each with a photo of their salesperson 'jockey' on their saddle. The progress of each sale was tracked by moving a horse over an obstacle on the racecourse and by listing each member of the team and their sales on a whiteboard.

This was all going swimmingly until a week before the end of the competition. One morning, the leading horse and jockey were gone from the racecourse and were nowhere to be found.

Soon after their disappearance was noticed, a whole company email was received. It was a ransom demand, complete with instructions on how the kidnapped horse could be recovered. For good measure, a 'proof of life' photo of the horse and jockey in front of that day's newspaper was included.

I cannot remember who took the horse or how the whole episode ended, but I do remember the great laugh it gave everyone in the organisation.

CASE STUDY – The anonymous team member

I have always treasured the lighter moments when they arrive, and I know I have a bias in favour of anyone who can make me laugh. The two things I enjoy the most in the world: the sound of my children's laughter and being helpless with laughter myself. Those magic moments of sharing a laugh with others help to build camaraderie, release tension and provide a defence against the absurdity that often surrounds us.

One of my favourite moments occurred during the first wave of the pandemic. From April 2020, my colleagues and I had moved to Microsoft Teams for all committee and board meetings. This was such an incredibly challenging and frightening time that laughter was the furthest thing from our minds. However, one sunny day, during a virtual committee meeting, we were able to find the funny.

All the meeting attendees were visible on the screen apart from one individual whose camera faced the sun, leaving him appearing as a shadowy outline against his background. We were on the final item, listening to the disembodied voice of our invisible colleague, when I could resist it no longer. I sent a message to my colleague who was chairing the meeting, asking, 'When did John join witness protection?'

I could see him struggling to keep it together as he ended the meeting with a little chuckle. I then received the reply: 'John, not his real name, told us...'

I rang him and we had a much needed and cathartic laugh to the point where we could not catch our breath. Whenever I think of this exchange, it still makes me smile.

Summary

This chapter has described how to develop and maintain resilience by:

- Setting goals
- Investing in your physical, mental and emotional health

- Spending time with inspirational ideas and people
- Laughing

The Firecracker Leader	The Poor Leader
• Sets personal goals aligned to organisational purpose	• Dismisses the need for personal goals
• Maintains personal health and wellbeing	• Fails to understand or invest in habits that sustain good health and wellbeing
• Finds effective methods to relax and recharge	
• Seeks inspiration in reading and learning	• Ignores the need for continuous learning and inspiration
• Uses positive self-talk	• Speaks negatively
• Accesses suitable mentors or coaches	• Takes advice from ill-qualified advisors
• Laughs often	• Is overly serious and rarely laughs

This chapter has covered the following Firecracker Leadership Framework attributes:

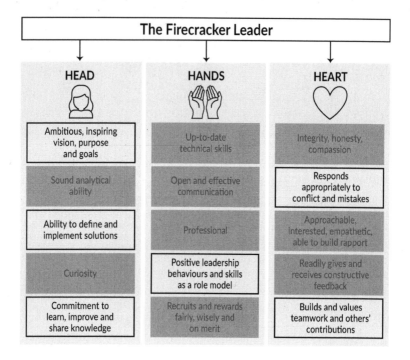

The Firecracker Leader		
HEAD	**HANDS**	**HEART**
Ambitious, inspiring vision, purpose and goals	Up-to-date technical skills	Integrity, honesty, compassion
Sound analytical ability	Open and effective communication	Responds appropriately to conflict and mistakes
Ability to define and implement solutions	Professional	Approachable, interested, empathetic, able to build rapport
Curiosity	Positive leadership behaviours and skills as a role model	Readily gives and receives constructive feedback
Commitment to learn, improve and share knowledge	Recruits and rewards fairly, wisely and on merit	Builds and values teamwork and others' contributions

References

1 N Hill, *Think and Grow Rich* (The Ralston Society, 1937)

2 R Black, 'Glossophobia (fear of public speaking): Are you glossophobic? Does speaking in public fill you with fear and anxiety? Try these tips for overcoming your fear of public speaking' (Psycom, 2019), www.psycom.net/glossophobia-fear-of-public-speaking, accessed 11 December 2023

3 Wonder Who, 'Actions speak louder than words: At least 70% of our communication is nonverbal' (2021), www.wonderwho.ch, accessed 8 January 2024

4 'Whatever the mind of man can conceive and believe, it can achieve.' N Hill, *Think and Grow Rich*, Preface (Napoleon Hill Foundation, 2020)

5   J Crump, 'Trump has narcissistic personality
    disorder, says leading psychoanalyst' (*The
    Independent*, 11 August 2020), www.independent.
    co.uk/news/world/americas/us-politics/
    donald-trump-narcissistic-personality-disorder-
    mary-trump-john-zinner-bandy-x-lee-a9665856.
    html, accessed 3 November 2023
6   Ibid
7   S Asma-Sadeque, 'Trump "deeply wounded
    narcissist" says former White House lawyer'
    (*The Guardian*, 10 Sept 2022), www.theguardian.
    com/us-news/2022/sep/10/trump-narcissist-
    white-house-lawyer-cbs, accessed 11 December
    2023
8   T Carter, *Coach Carter* (Paramount Pictures, 2005)
9   PCMLLC2012, 'Coach Carter I did that'
    (YouTube, May 2018), www.youtube.com/
    watch?v=qSN8nYqG-yA, accessed 11 December
    2023
10 'KPMG study finds 75% of female executives
    across industries have experienced imposter
    syndrome in their careers' (KPMG, 7 October
    2020) https://info.kpmg.us/news-perspectives/
    people-culture/kpmg-study-finds-most-female-
    executives-experience-imposter-syndrome.html,
    accessed 11 December 2023
11 Ibid
12 St. Jude Children's Research Hospital,
    'Leukemia in Children' (no date) www.stjude.
    org/disease/leukemia.html, accessed 5 January
    2024

13 D Atewologun, T Cornish and F Tresh, 'Unconscious bias training: An assessment of the evidence for effectiveness' (Equality and Human Rights Commission, Research report 113, March 2008), www.equalityhumanrights.com/sites/default/files/research-report-113-unconcious-bais-training-an-assessment-of-the-evidence-for-effectiveness-pdf.pdf, accessed 11 December 2023

14 D Carnegie, *How to Win Friends and Influence People* (Simon & Schuster, 1936)

15 Health Estates & Facilities Management Association, 'Calls for NHS Whistleblowing Review Following Lucy Letby Sentencing' (no date) www.hefma.co.uk/news/calls-for-nhs-whistleblowing-review-following-lucy-letby-sentencing, accessed 8 January 2024

16 Founders Online, 'From Thomas Jefferson to John Page, 15 July 1763' (National Archives, no date) https://founders.archives.gov/documents/Jefferson/01-01-02-0004, accessed 14 December 2023

17 Dr. Amit Ray, '101 Best Amit Ray Quotes' (no date) https://amitray.com/amitray-quotes, accessed 5 January 2024

18 Committee on Standards in Public Life, 'The seven principles of public life' (Gov.uk, 1995), www.gov.uk/government/publications/the-7-principles-of-public-life, accessed 11 December 2023

19 N Hill, *Think and Grow Rich* (Napoleon Hill Foundation, 1937)

20 SR Covey, *The 7 Habits of Highly Effective People: Powerful lessons in personal change* (Simon & Schuster, 2020)

21 N Hill, *Think and Grow Rich* (Napoleon Hill Foundation, 1937)

22 J Silva and P Miele, *The Silva Mind Control Method: The revolutionary program by the founder of the world's most famous mind control course* (Gallery, 2022)

23 The Pacific Institute®, www.thepacificinstitute. com, accessed 8 January 2024

24 Tony Robbins events, www.tonyrobbins.com, accessed 8 January 2024

25 J Rohn, *Seven Strategies for Wealth and Happiness* (Manjul Publishing House, 2009)

26 N Hill, *Think and Grow Rich* (Napoleon Hill Foundation, 1937)

27 Mayo Clinic Staff, 'Stress relief from laughter? It's no joke' (22 Sept 2023), www.mayoclinic. org/healthy-lifestyle/stress-management/ in-depth/stress-relief/art-20044456, accessed 11 December 2023

Further Reading

Bristol, CM and Sherman, H, *TNT: The power within you: How to release the forces inside you & get what you want* (Thorsons, 1992)

Brown, L, *Live Your Dreams* (Avon Books, 2000)

Bryson, B, *Notes From a Small Island* (Black Swan, 2015)

Carnegie, D, *How to Win Friends and Influence People* (Vermillion, 28th edition, 2006)

De Bono, E, *Six Thinking Hats: An essential approach to business management* (Little, Brown and Company, 1985)

Gawain, S, *Creative Visualization: Use the power of your imagination to create what you want in your life* (Embassy Books, 2020)

Harford, T, *How To Make The World Add Up: Ten rules for thinking differently about numbers* (Bridge Street Press, 2021)

Hay, L, *You Can Heal Your Life* (ReadHowYouWant, 2012)

Helmstetter, S, *What To Say When You Talk To Yourself: Powerful new techniques to programme your potential for success!* (Manjul, 2013)

Hill, N, *Think and Grow Rich* (Vermillion, updated edition, 2004)

Jeffers, S, *Feel The Fear and Do It Anyway* (Vermilion, 2019)

Lakhiani, V, *The 6 Phase Meditation Method: The proven technique to supercharge your mind, manifest your goals and make magic in minutes a day* (Rodale Books, 2022)

Paul, RW and Elder, L, 'Critical thinking: The nature of critical and creative thought' (*Journal of Developmental Education*, 30:2, 2006), www.semanticscholar.org/paper/Critical-Thinking%3A-The-Nature-of-Critical-and-Paul-Elder/8bc9e8bfe26e71fdf1cb68c93d7561c478d7c032, accessed 14 December 2023

Robbins, T, *Awaken The Giant Within: Take immediate control of your mental, emotional, physical and financial destiny* (Simon & Schuster, 2001)

Rohn, J, *Seven Strategies for Wealth and Happiness: Power ideas from America's foremost business philosopher* (Manjul, 2009)

Schwartz, DJ, *The Magic of Thinking Big* (Penguin, 2023)

Sinek, S, *Leaders Eat Last: Why some teams pull together and others don't* (Penguin, 2017)

Tice, L, *A Better World A Better You: The proven Lou Tice 'Investment In Excellence' program for achieving growth and success* (Pearson, 1989)

Tracy, B, *Goals: How to get everything you want – faster than you ever thought possible* (Berrett-Koehler, 2012)

Tracy, B, *The Psychology of Selling: Increase your sales faster and easier than you ever thought possible* (Thomas Nelson, 2006)

Wheelan, C, *Naked Statistics: Stripping the dread from the data* (WW Norton & Co, 2014)

Ziglar, Z, *Goals: How to get the most out of your life* (Sound Wisdom, 2019)

Acknowledgements

I would like to thank my family and friends for their constant encouragement, practical help and editorial feedback. Without them, I would never have completed this book. Thank you for believing in me.

I would like to thank all the colleagues and bosses I have had over the years for all the examples of leadership they have demonstrated and shared with me.

The Author

 Sue Musson achieved her first board-level leadership role at the age of twenty-seven. Since then, she has learned a thing or two about leadership which she is keen to share with others.

She has led numerous organisations, including her own successful businesses under the Firecracker brand. She recently established the Firecracker Foundation to help others fulfil their potential.

Sue has had the honour of serving for fifteen years as a non-executive director and chair of five of the UK's most significant healthcare organisations. She regularly chairs panels to appoint UK judges.

Sue is a dual citizen of the USA and the UK, speaking both languages fluently. She loves yoga, cricket, the Boston Red Sox and, most of all, spending time and laughing with her family and friends.

To learn more, visit:

🌐 www.suemusson.com

𝗂𝗇 www.linkedin.com/in/sue-musson-a0119416

◎ www.instagram.com/firecrackerleadership

▶ www.youtube.com/channel/ UCOKTL9tuURKl6P3Q6dYdYNw

♪ www.tiktok.com/@ firecrackerleader?_t=8ihHvD54n4K&_r=1